VH1 Music First **BEHIND THE MUSIC**™

teen idols

SARAH KELLY

POCKET BOOKS

New York   London   Toronto   Sydney   Singapore

ID040837

Many thanks to Jacob Hoye and Wendy Walker for letting me have so much fun with this. Thank you to Tommy Cody for his encouragement, support, encyclopedic knowledge of music and, of course, everything else.

The sale of this book without its cover is unauthorized. If you purchased this book without a cover, you should be aware that it was reported to the publisher as "unsold and destroyed." Neither the author nor the publisher has received payment for the sale of this "stripped book."

An *Original* Publication of VH1 Books/ Pocket Books

POCKET BOOKS, a division of Simon & Schuster, Inc.
1230 Avenue of the Americas, New York, NY 10020

Copyright © 2002 by Viacom International Inc. VH1: Music First, Behind the Music, and all related titles, logos, and characters are trademarks of Viacom International Inc.

All rights reserved, including the right to reproduce this book or portions thereof in any form whatsoever. For information address Pocket Books, 1230 Avenue of the Americas, New York, NY 10020

ISBN: 0-7434-2820-X

First VH1 Books/Pocket Books trade paperback printing February 2002

10 9 8 7 6 5 4 3 2 1

POCKET and colophon are registered trademarks of
Simon & Schuster, Inc.

Printed in the U.S.A.

For information regarding special discounts for bulk purchases, please contact
Simon & Schuster Special Sales at 1-800-456-6798 or business@simonandschuster.com

Tiffany seven-inch sleeve and record courtesy of MCA Records under license from Universal Music Enterprises. Andy Gibb seven-inch record courtesy of Polydor Records Ltd. (U.K.) under license from Universal Music Enterprises. Michael Ochs Archives.com (pages 8, 9, 10, 11, 14, 17, 20, 21, 22-23, 26, 27, 28, 30, 33, 35, 39, 40, 41, 42, 43, 45, 47, 49, 50, 52, 53, 54, 55, 56, 69, 74-75, 76, 78, 79, 80, 83, 93, 97, and 101-102). Harry Goodwin / Michael Ochs Archives.com (pages 25, 64-65, 66, 98-99). Waring Abbott / Michael Ochs Archives.com (pages 60, 62 and 63). Sherry Rayn Barnett / Michael Ochs Archives.com (pages 90 (top) and 91). Star File (pages 13, 59, 70-71). Star File / Jill Furmanovsky (pages 24 and 31). Star File / Bob Gruen (p. 18). Star File / Chuck Pulin (pages 89 and 110). Star File / Todd Kaplan (pages 82, 90 (bottom), 94, 103, 104, 105). Star File / Vinnie Zuffante (p. 108 - 109). Star File / Jon Mead (p. 92). Star File / Felix (p. 86). Star File / Beth Nussbaum (p. 73). Star File / Jeffrey Mayer (p. 106 - 107).

Cover photography: Todd Kaplan / Starfile (*NSYNC, Christina Aguilera).
Jon James / London Features International (Britney Spears).
W. Roelen / London Features International (Debbie Gibson). London Features International (Michael Jackson). Michael Ochs Archives.com (Rick Springfield, Leif Garrett).
Photofest (David Cassidy, Donny Osmond, Duran Duran).

Cover and interior design: Red Herring Design
Digital illustration: Malcolm Turk / www.Flickerinc.com

TABLE OF CONTENTS

"The screaming didn't stop... It was just a wall of hysteria."

BEHIND THE MUSIC:
TEEN IDOLS

If you love music and you've ever been a kid, chances are you've worshipped your share of pop stars. Clearly, your infatuation went beyond the way your idol looked or wore their hair, or that special way they held their guitar while they rocked out. More than any of that, it was about a certain time in your life. A time of innocence. A time of figuring out what you liked and what you didn't. A time when there was pure, clean excitement in having discovered something new, like a song you loved, and being allowed to just...love it.

The teen idol phenomenon came hand-in-hand with the conception of rock 'n' roll—the first music made expressly for teenagers. Girls were so wild about the hip-rocking, lip-curling Elvis that while he was off fighting for his country, lovesick fans were fighting for locks of his hair. In the '60s, John, Paul, Ringo, and George sent millions of young-sters into mass hysteria with every wave of their hands. Beatlemania wasn't just about selling records and #1 hits—it was also about crying and screaming so loud that even the Beatles couldn't hear themselves sing. Since then, the Fab Four have been the yardstick by which all other artists' success is measured.

There are all different kinds of teen idols. No two are created equal. A teen idol from the '70s singing golden oldies to sweet young things is very different from your '80s variety: artists straining to hear praise from critics over the shrieks of fourteen-year-olds. Some are marketed to land on lunch boxes, their careers designed by music moguls who know exactly what will make fans reach for their wallets. Others, in pursuit of becoming legitimate recording artists, with the good fortune of a beautiful face and a few catchy hooks, suddenly find themselves in the pages of *Tiger Beat*. These are the reluctant idols. Either way, teen adoration is undiscerning. Once an artist is on top, it hardly seems important to the fan how he got there.

Behind the Music: Teen Idols is a select collection of pop stars past and present whose ascent to fame was fueled by teen worship, love, and money—thereby branding them teen idols forever. Whether they had actual musical credibility or not wasn't important; they were defined solely by their audience, and often there's no escaping that.

Though some of these artists became teen idols well after their own adolescent years, most of them hit it big while still kids themselves and found it difficult to grow out of that role as they grew up. The transition from pop pinup to legit musician is never an easy one. These stories encapsulate the rise and fall—and in some rare cases, rise again—of a sampling of the most cherished idols of the last thirty years.

Chances are there's someone in here you once loved. With *all* your heart. So don't be bashful. Pull out your copy of Leif Garrett's "I Was Made for Dancing" or "Jessie's Girl" by Rick Springfield. Throw on the Partridge Family's "I Think I Love You" or the Bay City Rollers' "Shang-a-Lang." And get ready to fall in love all over again. ✿

CHAPTER 1

THE EVOLUTION OF THE TEEN IDOL

A Brief History

Before the invention of rock 'n' roll, teenagers listened dutifully to their parents' music. Elvis, much to the dismay of mothers and fathers everywhere, changed all that and teens worldwide became devoted converts. In the years that followed, as newcomers arrived at the party, it became clear to record companies, managers, and promoters how much bang they could get for the teen buck. Here's a look at some of the performers who, with every record set and every fan earned, taught them all a thing or two. In other words, they're some of the working models for teen idol success.

ELVIS PRESLEY

In the mid-1950s, Memphis native Elvis appeared on the music scene simmering with sexuality, matinee idol looks, and a kind of song that had never been heard by the masses before. Instantly, Elvis's rock 'n' roll became a phenomenal success with teenagers, and their support was evidenced in his record-breaking achievements—the King held court on the charts from 1956 to around 1964, when he had to share that piece of prime real estate with the Beatles.

His stage antics—the sashaying hips, slicked-back pompadour, and the overt sexuality of it all—tapped into something that had been missing in music, and similarly, something kids of the '50s weren't supposed to acknowledge. His performances were characterized by audience frenzy, a mania, a purely emotional reaction to what was happening onstage. What's more was that his popularity was able to spread with another new medium: television. More than 40 million viewers were estimated to catch him performing "Heartbreak Hotel," "Shake, Rattle and Roll," and "Blue Suede Shoes" on *The Milton Berle Show* in April 1956. A now-legendary appearance on *The Ed Sullivan Show* filmed the King from the waist up so as not to offend the good people of America with his gyrating lower half.

But the kids weren't having any of it. They pledged their allegiance to this rock 'n' roll icon by purchasing his records by the millions, paying for tickets to see his movies, and granting him 22 Top Ten hits by 1960.

JERRY LEE LEWIS

Dubbed the Killer by his own mother, Jerry Lee Lewis was a piano-playing southern rocker with a big attitude. Dick Clark even called him "one of the founding fathers of rock 'n' roll." In 1956, at twenty-one years old, Lewis recorded a demo tape at Sun Studios, the same place where Elvis had recorded his first hits. His 1957 debut single, "Whole Lot of Shakin' Going On," was virtually banned by radio because it was deemed too sexually charged. But when the Killer sang it on TV's *Steve Allen Show,* both he and the song became an instant success—within three days, radio stations across the country were playing it.

Lewis's renegade style attracted the attention of girls everywhere. He was a live wire, a supercharged dose of adrenaline when he performed, and his fans found him irresistible. When he sang "Great Balls of Fire" on *American Bandstand* in November 1957, it was easy to see that he had that winning combination of riotous rock 'n' roll and infectious personality. "Kids loved him because they'd never seen anybody perform like that. You looked out [at the audience]—people were going crazy—talking about it the next day. And you knew he was huge," says Clark.

But with every rise there must be a fall, and Lewis's came when he married his second cousin, Myra, in December 1957. She was only thirteen at the time, and Lewis wasn't even divorced from his second wife yet. A scandal ensued and knocked the rocker off the charts for three years. By the time he staged a comeback, America's attention had already turned to four mop-headed boys from Liverpool.

THE BEATLES

Any pop group who's made it relatively big in the last thirty-five years may have, at one point or another, likened themselves to the Beatles. The minute a band gets more than five thousand fans screaming its name, it's Beatlemania all over again. In the early '60s, fans signed up by the thousands, catapulting the Fab Four—John Lennon, Paul McCartney, George Harrison, and Ringo Starr—into a kind of superstardom that had never before existed. They went from playing small clubs to stadium arenas, where the screaming got so loud you couldn't even hear them sing.

John Lennon once said in an interview that the band's ambition was to be bigger than Elvis. "At first we wanted to be bigger than Goffin and King, then we wanted to be Eddie Cochran, then Buddy Holly, but finally we arrived at wanting to be bigger than the biggest—Elvis Presley." And with a string of 1964 hits ("I Want to Hold Your Hand," "She Loves You," "Please Please Me," and "Twist and Shout"), it was easy to see that they'd have no problem getting there.

Among the many firsts credited to the Beatles was the widespread mania among teens. Ringo recalled one 1963 show where "we were in a cage... because it got so crazy. It was like being in a zoo, on stage. It felt dangerous. The kids were out of hand. It was the first time I felt that if they got near us we would be ripped apart."

In their seven-plus years together, the Beatles changed the course of pop music forever—not only in terms of the music they were making and the records achieved but also in the context of how far their fans would go to prove their love and utter devotion. Beatlemania went so far that it became an international movement, an indelible part of history, a beast unto itself. Paul once said, "The thing is, we never believed in Beatlemania, never took the whole thing that seriously. I suppose that way we managed to stay sane."

BOBBY SHERMAN

With his Southern California good looks and catchy pop numbers, Sherman symbolized a sign of things to come for teen idols in the '70s and '80s. He got his break in 1964 on the rock 'n' roll TV show *Shindig!* He then went on to make his mark on the charts with bubblegum tunes like 1969's "Little Woman" and "La La La (If I Had You)," and 1970's "Easy Come, Easy Go" and "Julie, Do Ya Love Me"—all of which made it into the Top Ten. His successful run was an invitation to such teen idols as Rex Smith, David Cassidy, Donny Osmond, and Leif Garrett to join the party. At the height of his popularity, Sherman's face was a fixture on the teen magazines that had begun to infiltrate America. Though his career as a teen idol was short-lived, it was nonetheless proof that there was not only a strong demand for teenybopper music, but also for any kind of fan appreciation outlet available—whether it be through magazines, merchandise, or other memorabilia. To this day, that's one thing that hasn't changed. ✿

"It happened so quickly, and I remember thinking it was just a job. I wanted to pay the rent. That's all. I didn't think that I would be on television, they'd be making comic books and lunch boxes—I didn't even think about any of it. I was nineteen, trying to pay the rent. I thought, well, that's cool. I've got another month's rent done." —DAVID

Prince in Pooka Shells

B y the end of *The Partridge Family*'s four-year run on television, David Cassidy could do more than pay the rent. He had accumulated six gold albums and seven Top 40 hits with his fictional TV family, had played to hundreds of thousands of fans in live shows worldwide, his name was on the lips of teenage girls everywhere, and his face decorated their bedroom walls. The fact that the show's first single, "I Think I Love You," went to #1 on the pop charts before the first episode had even aired made it clear that David Cassidy was about to become big business.

After graduating high school, he paid the bills with small roles on shows like *Adam 12*, *Bonanza,* and *Marcus Welby, M.D.*, before landing the role of Keith Partridge at the age of nineteen. Having always been passionate about music, this seemed a perfect fit for an actor about to play a pop star. "I had been to see Clapton and Hendrix and B.B. King, and these were my musical influences at the time," he says. "And I was a big fan of R&B...I had no idea what the music was going to be, because it hadn't been created yet. So I envisioned it as being like a rock band. I'm nineteen, you know, I'm thinking, this is cool. I can make this happen."

"They never this is kind of to somebody's

In fact, David was hired only to act. For that he'd get paid a modest six hundred dollars per week. Accomplished session musicians were to provide the behind-the-scenes tunes for the show, and the fresh-faced Partridges would lip-synch and act like they knew how to play their instruments. The only cast member with a musical background was acclaimed Broadway actress Shirley Jones, David's stepmother, who, unbeknownst to him, had been hired to play his mother on the show. The two ran into each other at David's audition, each just as surprised as the other.

But it was no accident that David would

become a huge star from playing Keith Partridge. "We were looking for a kid who could be that guy. Who was going to get on the cover of *Tiger Beat* and every other magazine," says Paul Junger-Witt, the show's producer. What TV execs didn't bank on was David's voice, which, as it turned out, was simply dreamy.

"They never asked me if I could sing," says David. So he convinced the producers to audition him in the studio. He says he told his manager that "this is kind of silly for me to be lip-syncing to somebody's voices. I'm a singer and I play." He explained to the producers "that I had been in rock 'n' roll bands and that I'd sung on Broadway and that I'd

he was just singing the lyrics, he seemed like he felt what he was singing about. But more importantly, his image and his look—the perfect teeth, the early '70s hair, the clean-cut teen-idol looks, I think that all went with it too. I think people fell for the whole package."

THEY THINK THEY LOVE YOU

When the series made its debut on September 25, 1970, it became an overnight success, both on the pop charts and in the Nielsen ratings. Fans whole-

asked me if I could sing... silly for me to be lip-synching voice. I'm a singer and I play."

been the soloist in the choir from the time I was five years old." His audition was proof that he had the chops, and it was all he needed to lay down vocals on the first single.

Says Shirley Jones, "He had this wonderful, sensitive quality in his voice. And a very sort of young, breathy sound that was so great, and of course, the girls all agreed. I mean, they all went crazy when they heard him sing. And I could understand why."

Barry Scott, host of *The Lost 45s*, a radio program dedicated to Top 40 hits of the '70s and '80s, attributes David's success as Partridge frontman to the fact that he "seemed to, for young teenage girls, emote. It didn't seem like

heartedly embraced (and that's putting it mildly) a show about a wholesome family of troubadours, their upbeat, puppy-love inspired music, and most especially, David's alter ego, brother Keith.

As Shirley Jones remembers, they "were all in shock when 'I Think I Love You' became the hit that it was. We had no idea that this was going to happen. We knew we had nice music. We knew we had David Cassidy. He was good looking, and talented and wonderful. We knew we had a great family and everybody was going to do a good job. But the phenomenon of the music and David becoming the number-one star in America at that point, nobody knew that that was going to happen. The fact that the first song just went off the charts was a real shock to everybody. Happily we were thrilled. But, it was amazing that it happened."

15

"I Think I Love You" was followed on the charts by two straight Top Ten singles: "Doesn't Somebody Want to Be Wanted" in February 1971, and "I'll Meet You Halfway" in May of that same year. The reason for such instant success is as simple to crack as that ubiquitous partridge egg in the show's opening. *Partridge Family* session drummer Hal Blaine explains: "The music that we were making with and for the Partridge Family—we referred to it as 'bubblegum' in those days. It was kind of young lyrics, young people, and that entire show was oriented toward the youngsters....It was not sophisticated, the songs were not major love songs. They were cute, young kids' love songs, if you will." Love songs that became all the lovelier because they were sung by David Cassidy. According to keyboardist Mike Melvoin, "there's a certain formula for rock 'n' roll success. And the vulnerable young boy is a rock 'n' roll formula."

Teenagers went absolutely wild for David. Carrot-topped co-star Danny Bonaduce, who played Keith Partridge's mischievous younger brother, could not only see what his overwhelming appeal was, he also felt the same way. "David Cassidy was a god," says Bonaduce. "That's why I idolized him, because he was an idol....The guy was, I mean, he is and was stellar handsome. I mean the guy is gorgeous to look at....Perfect hair, bitchin' little pooka shells, and chicks just dug him. What was there not to idolize about this guy? It was great. So anything David Cassidy liked, I liked. Anything David Cassidy didn't like, I didn't like."

At the start of the show's second season, the Partridge Family scored its fourth straight Top 20 hit, "I Woke Up in Love This Morning," followed shortly after by its fifth, "It's One of Those Nights (Yes Love)." Things couldn't have looked better for David. His star was on the rise and girls couldn't get enough of him (read his autobiography and you'll see what we mean). He recalls what it was like just to get to work everyday: "Down in the front of the lot every morning there were lots of fans. And I would have to go down over there as you drove up to the gate, I would have to find different ways in. So I would have to meet somebody to change cars with me. Come in a different gate, go out a different gate. Because I couldn't get in, as of the second year, third year, fourth year."

A PARTRIDGE IN A QUANDARY

As the show became increasingly popular, and the music kept hitting those high notes, the show's execs found ways to capitalize on their boy wonder. David's was suddenly the face that launched thousands of lunch boxes, Thermoses, toothbrushes, T-shirts— you name it, they bought it. The demand for David and anything bearing his likeness was unrelenting. There was no such thing as too much when it came to those baby blues. But David wasn't aware at that point the extent to which he was being marketed. The huge crowds of teenage girls he drew every time he stepped foot outside the studio lot kept him from living a normal life, and for the most part, those crowds kept him isolated.

"I'm on the set every day, I'm in the studio at night, and there's all this madness going on around me," David says about the show's early days. "People taking photographs,

DAVID4EVER

"When I was nine or ten years old, I was attracted to David Cassidy at first because of his looks. Then when he would sing, I felt as though he was only singing to me. Of course, so did a lot of other girls! I would get my mom to buy anything that had his name or face on it. So I have a big collection of old stuff—magazines, lunch box, Viewmaster reel set, puzzle, all the records—you name it. I now have a bigger collection because he's back. I saw him in concert in 1990 in Pontiac, Michigan, for his comeback tour. I still had the same butterflies I had way back when." —VICKI, THIRTY-EIGHT

people telling me I'm going to be the next coming of Jesus, and you know, it feels really cool to be getting all this attention. Suddenly, everybody likes me, everybody loves me. And I'm not aware because I don't go into stores. I'm not aware that they're manufacturing David Cassidy T-shirts and dresses and bubble-gum cards and comic books and writing books about my life that are all fabricated."

The most disturbing part for David was the fact that he was becoming synonymous with Keith Partridge. To his fans, the two heart-throbs were one and the same. "It bothered me," David says, "because they were creating an image that wasn't real. So I went and talked to the teen magazines, and I said, 'Come on, this isn't real'.... They looked at me and patted me on the back. I said, 'Take me off the covers of these magazines.' And they went, 'I don't think so.'"

He was being sold to teenagers as the fun-loving, sometimes goofy Keith, the kid who always wanted to borrow the keys to the tour bus—an image that couldn't have been further from the real David Cassidy. He was playing a sixteen-year-old guitar-toting kid when he was actually nineteen; he and his friends, who were products of the socially and politically conscious 1960s, were listening to Jimi Hendrix, the Doors, Buffalo Springfield, and the Velvet Underground, while David-as-Keith was "making pop commercial records." He remembers thinking, "My friends aren't going to think I'm very cool anymore." And though he welcomed the fame and attention his Partridge Family hits were bringing, his musical tastes were not reflected in them at all.

"That was my frustration," says David. "Every person on the planet perceived David Cassidy as that's who I was. Not only was I playing Keith but there I was singing, and that was my voice and that must be my musical taste. So it was in a sense being robbed of your own identity. And, of who you are, because of the great, tremendous success of the character I was playing and the music I was playing as that character."

> "The naivete of the time promoted a real distance, like stars were bigger than life.
>
> # I was bigger than life.
>
> And all of the marketing and merchandising did exactly that. There were books and dresses and comic books and magazines and bubblegum cards. Making this persona that they had really created— and that I was perpetuating every week on television— bigger than life."

COME ON, GET HAPPY ALREADY!

At his manager's suggestion, David found a way to remedy the situation—by embarking on a solo tour while still taping *The Partridge Family*. Fans came out by the thousands to glimpse at their piece of pop perfection in person, and hear his own brand of rock 'n' roll. "I think the first date was in Seattle,

and Portland. I was playing the first couple dates for like, I think 8,000, 10,000, and then it went to 15,000 a night. And then it became 25,000 a night, 50,000 a night as it evolved," he says. "And I'd make you know, $50,000, $60,000, $70,000 a day. So what I made on the television show was, like, nothing. Those numbers are big now, but they were astronomical in those days. Astronomical. No one made that kind of money. I was making more money than Elvis was. I was playing to more people than he was at the time. So, I'm not comparing me to him, I'm just telling you, in retrospect, at the time, for those four years, five years, those were the numbers that I was dealing with."

Between touring and the show, David had created a grueling schedule for himself. By the time he was twenty-one, he was playing three sold-out shows a day on weekends, and reporting to the set of the TV show weekdays. Cast members could see how exhausted David was, and the toll that the nonstop mania was taking on him. By the third season, he was growing increasingly disenchanted with his role as Keith Partridge, and most especially, the fact that the show's music had not evolved—as in, the bubblegum had gone stale. The differences between David and Keith were becoming harder to reconcile. After all, as he puts it, there are only so many times you can ask your TV mom to borrow the keys to the bus.

David was also becoming worn down by the teen-idol image that had helped perpetuate his larger-than-life status. He says he often found himself feeling "very uncomfortable with feeling good about the fact that there were lots of kids, teenagers that really looked upon me as a role model. And I think I was a pretty good one. I always took that very seriously. Because obviously if you have an influence on people, particularly on kids, I was more concerned about the effect that it would have if they were to be aware of who I was, what I was, what I really was as opposed to what they had been brainwashed with, how perhaps shocked they would be."

By that point, Shirley Jones recalls, "David did not want to be Keith Partridge by a long shot. He didn't like the music, he thought it was too bubblegum for him. He was in a place at that point in time where he wanted to be a rock star. And we were not a rock family. And Keith Partridge was certainly not a rock star. So he felt that that was certainly not him."

David found himself, during the third season of the show, ready to move on. Record buyers were not as interested in the next Partridge Family single as they had been, though David's stock was still pretty high. After a kidnapping threat, which forced him to move into a hotel for a month and retain a hired guard, David's reality intensified. "I was so frightened by the concept that I was going to end up being Elvis or this teen has-been, somehow or another I had to let the world finally see that there was more to me than just this commercial, glossy image."

In early 1974, the fourth season of America's beloved *Partridge Family*, David announced he'd be saying goodbye to his TV brothers and sisters. At twenty-three, he decided it was finally time to move on and shed his Keith Partridge persona. The decision wasn't made overnight. "It was over a period of time," says David, "and I became more and more withdrawn. I became more and more empty. My life felt like it had no meaning to it. I felt taken by the machine. I felt abused. I felt burnt out emotionally, physically, and I really thought, you know, I've done this experience like no one's ever done it. Or as well as anyone's ever done it. There's nothing more that I can make out of it. I could keep doing concerts, I could keep doing this, but if you ever want to get on with your life, boy, you've got to do something else, and you've got to get back to finding out what that is." The final episode of the show aired on August 31, 1974.

20

GOING SO-LOW

David would keep at his solo career for a short while after, but he'd never recapture the frenzied roller-coaster ride that carried him through his initial shot at fame. In the late '70s, he went back to TV acting, as a policeman in NBC's *David Cassidy— Man Undercover,* a series that lasted only thirteen weeks. He went through two failed marriages, the first to actress Kay Lenz in 1977, and the second to Meryl Tanz in 1984. He also tried his hand in Broadway shows, taking on roles in *Joseph and the Amazing Technicolor Dreamcoat,* and a touring production of *Jesus Christ Superstar.* (And much later, in 1993, he starred with half brother and teen idol in his own right, Shaun Cassidy, in Broadway's *Blood Brothers*). Like others who've been catapulted at an early age to worldwide fame and the money that goes with it, David found himself down and out in the early '80s, drinking heavily and over eight hundred thousand dollars in debt. With the help of therapy, and the determination to save himself from personal and financial ruin, David pulled himself out of that rut and put his career back together again. In the mid-'80s David, now married to songwriter Sue Schrifin, once again thrust himself into the music scene.

After a chance radio appearance during which David sang three of his new songs, he was signed to the record company Enigma, and subsequently recorded an eponymous new album. A year later, his single "Lyin' to Myself" went to #27 on the pop charts. He also took the stage at the MGM Grand in Las Vegas in 1996 and went on to be the bestselling show on the strip.

Without a doubt, *The Partridge Family* holds a nostalgic place in the American cultural memory. That psychedelic bus, the infectious, light-as-air pop songs, the fresh-faced cast, the all-American heart-throb in hip-huggers who captured the hearts of adoring young fans—all part of a phenomenon that came along at exactly the right time.

"My listeners are very enthusiastic about the Partridge Family," says Barry Scott of *The Lost 45s.* "I think because it represents a very happy time in their life. A time when they had little worries, other than homework or which lunch box to take to school. And now that they're adults, I think they can look back fondly upon that period and smile and say, 'Hey, that song is kind of cute'."

Now having gained some perspective on the whirlwind of his teen-idol superstardom, David says, "I never had any bitterness or ill feelings about it. Because I truly knew that I had done something that was extraordinary. And that when you make millions of people around the world happy, when you bring light and joy and enlightenment for whatever, however you want to look at it, it brought people together." ✿

CHAPTER 3

The Jackson

Dancing Machines

I t's hard to believe the King of Pop got his start at the opening of a Big Top Supermarket. The grand opening. And it wasn't just Michael Jackson—his brothers Jackie, Jermaine, Tito, and Marlon headlined the supermarket as well. Everybody has to start somewhere, and when the youngest member of the band isn't much older than five, it's as good a place to start as any. And by the time that gig was done, they were already on the express register line to stardom.

The Jackson brothers were five in a family of nine children growing up in Gary, Indiana. Their father, Joe, was a steelworker and a blues guitarist. By some accounts, he was also a strict disciplinarian, who, like the head of the Osmond household, was dedicated to making stars of his boys. Beginning in 1962, the fivesome honed their act in local clubs. Michael was four then, and Jackie, the oldest, was eleven. They officially became a group in 1964, entering talent shows and contests, and becoming frequent openers for other acts. Success came quickly for the young-

...sters— they went from winning a talent contest at Harlem's famed Apollo Theater in 1966 to opening for Gladys Knight & the Pips the following year. With Michael as their frontman, the Jackson 5 became known for their charismatic performances, upbeat blend of R&B and pop music, and playful yet tight choreography. It was easy to see how the group, with a lead singer not even in the double digits, made such a favorable impression on their early audiences. In no time at all, the brothers landed a record contract with the Indiana-based Steeltown label, and put a few tracks down on tape. But the boys wouldn't stay there long.

By the middle of 1968, after seeing an audition tape of the Jackson 5, Berry Gordy signed the burgeoning idols to a one-year deal with Motown. And what a deal it was—for Motown that is: each Jackson would earn less than half a cent for every single, and two cents per album. For every song recorded, they'd get $12.50—but only if it was released.

Shortly after, Gordy moved the whole Jackson family out to Hollywood to prep them for superstardom. They were on their way.

THE ABCS OF SWEET SUCCESS

Diana Ross Presents the Jackson 5, the group's first album, came out in 1969 and it earned them their first #1 single, "I Want You Back." Originally written for Gladys Knight & the Pips, the track was overhauled for the young Jacksons, and it became the fastest-selling record in Motown history at the time. In October 1969, they appeared on TV's *Hollywood Palace*, and a couple of months later, turned in a performance on *The Ed Sullivan Show*, a rite of passage for musical acts at the time. Over the next nine months, they'd release a second album, *ABC*, and reach the #1 spot three more times with such instant classics as "ABC," "The Love You Save," and "I'll Be There."

Responsible for writing their early music was "the Corporation"—a prolific group of Motown hit-makers with a spot-on formula for success. If the Osmond Brothers were scoring big with their brand of bubblegum-sweetened rock, the Jackson 5 cornered

The Jackson 5 cornered the market on a different kind of sound— an irresistible fusion of soul-grabbing R&B and kid-friendly pop.

the market on a different kind of sound—an irresistible fusion of soul-grabbing R&B and kid-friendly pop.

What the two family-oriented groups did share was space on the covers of teeny-bopper magazines. Youngsters around the country were dying for an eyeful of Motown's youngest sensations. Soon enough, fans got their wish in the form of the Jackson 5's 1971 TV special, *Goin' Back to Indiana.* That same year, "Mama's Pearl" and "Never Can Say Goodbye" both went to #2, and the boys packed their bags for a U.S. tour. And in the midst of all that, thirteen-year-old Michael was launching a career independent of his older brothers. While the Jackson 5's music struck a chord with audiences of all ages— not only teens—young Michael's solo act, on the other hand, was like an aerogram delivered straight to the hearts of the under-sixteen set. His first outing landed him a #4 spot on the charts with "Got to Be There."

Michael tugged at the heartstrings of girls everywhere with songs like "I Wanna Be Where You Are" and "Ben," a movie theme song that was originally meant for teen rival Donny Osmond to record. And, as if the Jackson machine wasn't already working in overdrive, a Saturday morning cartoon series starring the brothers ran weekly on TV. Also, in late 1972, encouraged by Michael's solo success, Jermaine released his first single, "That's How Love Goes." The Jackson 5 seemed to be churning out a new record every year (1971's *Goin' Back to Indiana* and *Maybe Tomorrow*, 1972's *Looking Through the Windows*). By this point, the Corporation was no longer penning the J5 hits, and the group experimented with '50s remakes and covers of songs like Jackson (no relation) Browne's "Doctor My Eyes," as well as recording some original material of their own.

On top of all that, the Jacksons, who were internationally adored, added touring to their already busy schedule. They rode the wave of fame around the world to places as far-reaching as Hawaii, Africa, and Australia, where they made history as the first major African-American group to tour the country. The Jackson 5 wasn't immune to the mania that was characteristic of the teen idol boom in the early '70s. In fact, a 1974 U.K. tour was canceled when Joe Jackson accidentally revealed the group's ETA at Heathrow Airport to a newspaper. Gordy, who had concerns about security and was fearful in the wake of the death of a David Cassidy fan at a concert in London, put the kibosh on the British gigs.

Outside of touring, the brothers' steady hit singles kept them wildly popular for the next few years. By 1975, the Jackson 5 was writing and producing the bulk of their records, and when their contract with Motown expired that year, they defected to Epic. (That is, everyone but Jermaine, who was by then married to Gordy's daughter and so remained with Motown. He was replaced in the family lineup by fifteen-year-old brother Randy.) Motown was none too pleased, but then again, neither were the Jacksons. All told, they had recorded 469 songs for the label, and out of those, only 174 were released. And in the face of so much success, so many chart-topping hits, they walked away with just 2.7 percent in royalties.

The following year, a dismayed Gordy sued the brothers for breach of contract and the brothers sued back. To add insult to injury, they found out that Gordy had

And in the face of so much success, so many chart-topping hits, they walked away with only 2.7 percent in royalties.

taken out a patent on their name, so they were forced to become, simply, the Jacksons. The case was finally settled four years later, with the brothers forking over six hundred thousand dollars.

DON'T STOP 'TILL YOU GET ENOUGH— AND EVEN THEN...

The latter half of the '70s found the Jacksons enjoying the concurrent success of their solo careers as well as their group efforts. The disco craze was in full swing and the brothers did it just as well as anyone else. "Enjoy Yourself" and "Shake Your Body (Down to the Ground)" both boogied into the Top Ten, and Michael's "Rock With You" and "Don't Stop 'Till You Get Enough" didn't quit until they reached #1.

By the time 1980 rolled around, the oldest member was nearly thirty and Michael was already twenty-two. Hardly teens anymore, the group had grown up and was entering a new phase. Michael—on the verge of his "Billie Jean"/"Thriller" silver-gloved era—was well on his way to his coronation as pop royalty. Once there, his fame, fans, and success would far surpass what he'd enjoyed as a teen idol—in fact, to call his post-Jackson 5 career a phenomenon would be an understatement. The Jacksons continued to perform together for several years, but clocked in their last couple of chart hits in 1984, which included "State of Shock," featuring that other iconic MJ— Mick Jagger. That year's Victory Tour was the last Jacksons concert event that featured Michael. Tickets went for thirty dollars.

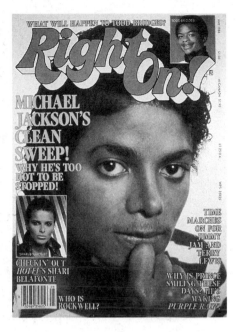

While some folks continue to wax nostalgic about the heyday of the Jackson 5, Michael's fans are still in the millions worldwide. In fact, if you were among the lucky, you could have caught the New York City tribute to the King of Pop in September 2001 that reunited him with brothers Jermaine, Jackie, Tito, Marlon, and Randy. But you would have needed more than thirty dollars for that one. Much, much more. The highest priced tickets rang in at twenty-five hundred dollars a pop. ✿

CHAPTER 4

And They Called It Puppy Love

DONNY OSMOND

Donny Came to My House! WARNING!!

IF U LUV ME DON'T TURN TO PAGE 22 *Donny Gives You Hawaii* Is Donny Losing You?

OSMONDS: RED-HOT LOVERS *Donny's Secret Room* Donny: What He Won't Tell!

So go the headlines from teenybopper magazines like *Tiger Beat* and *SPeC*, circa 1972–73. From the sound of it, at fifteen years old Donny Osmond was the original international man of mystery.

See, it's hard work being a teen idol. You have to be so many things to so many girls. Sweet-faced boy next door. Secretive seducer.

Someone who can offer the world and make all your prepubescent dreams come true. Someone who can give you Hawaii.

With Top Ten gold hits like "Sweet and Innocent," "Go Away Little Girl," and "Puppy Love," Donny was the ultimate sensitive kid girls fell for. In show business from the time he was six, Donny was already a seasoned pro by the time the mania hit, with an established career and a knack for making even adults swoon. His chubby cheeks, big white smile, and genuine sweetness were hard to resist—or escape, for that matter. He fit the part until his reign was up, and by then the part didn't fit him anymore. And that's when the hardest work of all came.

HEY LITTLE DONNY

One of nine children born to devout Mormons George and Olive Osmond, Donny made his debut in Ogden, Utah, in December 1957. As Donny was learning to walk and talk, four of his older brothers created a barbershop quartet, honing their act during family nights. A chance meeting in Disneyland landed the boys a contract to appear in "Disneyland After Dark," which eventually led to a regular gig on the weekly *Andy Williams Show* on NBC. The Osmond Brothers, in the true spirit of what it means to be a family act, had young Donny belting out tunes alongside them by the time he was six. He sang solo, though, the first time he was on the show, performing "You Are My Sunshine." Hearts melted across the country.

Success at such a young age came with its pressures for the brothers. Says Donny, "We were known as the 'one-take Osmonds' to the point where we were really hard on ourselves if we didn't get it in one take." Adds brother Jay: "Donny grew up with [the idea] that his job was to please everybody and be perfect."

Shortly after the *Andy Williams Show* ended its five-year run, the Osmond Brothers fivesome—Alan, Wayne, Merrill, Jay, and Donny—scored a record deal. In 1969, they got together with producer Mike Curb, who wanted to position the group like another popular quintet—the Jackson 5. "We purposely copied the Jackson 5 on the first record *One Bad Apple*," Curb says. His method worked, and the single shot to #1 on the U.S. charts in January 1971.

The teen magazines swooped in and Donny became their poster boy. Straightaway, millions of girls pined for him. "It was something similar to Beatlemania," recalls Curb. The demand for the littlest Osmond brother was so great that Curb pushed him toward a solo album to satiate his fans' appetites. Donny did just that and released *The Donny Osmond Album* that same year.

> **"The unfortunate thing is that my solo career...just came to totally overshadow the music my brothers and I were making.... I was recording the tender love ballads, and the Osmonds were doing rock songs like 'Crazy Horses,' and there were two commercial impulses pulling at our group."**
>
> —DONNY, ON DONNY.COM

The first single, "Go Away Little Girl," flew to #1. Now that Donny was front and center stage, his hit song overshadowed the Osmond Brothers, and all adoring eyes were fixed on him, and him alone.

But Donny continued to perform with the group, touring the world, bringing fans in by the thousands, and causing mass hysteria wherever they went. The Osmond Brothers and Donny on his own soared up the pop charts with single after single. It was a big business for the family, and behind the sweet smiles and sugary, bubblegum tunes, they took it very seriously. "That was a lifestyle to us," says Donny. "We didn't know any other way because we'd been in show business ever since we were practically born. When the adulation hit in the early '70s, it was just the next step in the evolution of a career and so it wasn't anything abnormal to me or to any of us."

Nothing abnormal? Think again.

"I remember Zeppelin came to see a show once," says younger sister Marie, recalling some of the insanity at the brothers' shows. "And they looked at this sound, they were measuring the decibels and our show was much louder than Zeppelin, just to get over the screams of the girls....I remember going to Heathrow Airport and I was standing there with my brothers, and I watched the whole balcony collapse because of the weight of the girls. So we were banned from Heathrow. It was hysteria."

Donny recalls a show in Akron, Ohio: "We were in kind of like a concave stage—terrible design. Wooden picket fence in front of the stage. So all these girls started rushing the stage during the show, because I'd throw out this Donny cap—I used to wear the Donny cap, and I'd throw two or three of them out. Terrible thing to do. As soon as I threw one out, people started rushing the stage. Well, the bad part about it was that this wooden picket fence couldn't hold all of that force, and it started breaking, and people were getting severely hurt. We had to shut the show down. But a lot of the fans were very clever. They saw that people were being pulled up onstage because... it was the only way to get them out....So a lot of girls were pretending to faint to get pulled up onstage. And there was this one girl, hats off to her, man, she was so smart. She got pulled up onstage, and she was just out, in a coma. As soon as she was onstage, she came to life and darted over to me, and held onto me, and wouldn't let go."

You'd think it would be virtually impossible for a teenage boy with a hit record career, a couple of #1 hits holding up his bell-bottoms, and girls crying their hearts out for him, to keep everything in perspective. He says,

"You start believing the hype, and I think that's why now I can look back with a little bit more of an appreciation for my parents, and the family that we came from, that they kept our feet on the ground despite the fact that there were screaming girls after us all the time. I mean that was so much fun, you know, but when we'd go home we were family, we had family night, family home evening."

> **"My job for a long time was keeping track of fan mail and I would go over and open letters and they'd all say, 'Donny, I love you and I've had this dream and I'm going to marry you.'"**
> —MARIE OSMOND

Being cute and lovable came with its pressures too. Aside from the hard work of touring and constantly performing, there was emotional stress as well. "The first time I had to be perfect in a bad way was when I was thirteen years old," Donny recalls. "I was in all the fan magazines, and everything I did ended up in print. Everything I said was sometimes taken out of context. People would come up to me and say, 'How dare you say something like that.' Well, then I had to be perfect."

In retrospect, he says, "If I had to point to one thing and say that's the reason why

"I don't know how my parents kept us from getting the big head because, boy, you know, when you have that much adoration and fan mail and things like that, I imagine it could go to your head. There was a time when I was about eighteen years old. I wasn't pompous, I wasn't egotistical, but I thought, 'this is starting to get really easy....'"

—DONNY

I didn't flip out, and that I'm halfway normal, well, actually there's two things. One would be my faith and my belief in God. And number two it's my wife because, despite the fact that I had a great foundation to fall back on, it didn't exempt me from any emotional problems that come from that kind of a career. That doesn't solve loneliness. It doesn't solve being a teen idol and then it doesn't solve having your career go into the toilet. It doesn't solve any of those things....I needed companionship, because you know, you think Donny Osmond—all these screaming girls and this kind of stuff—and the last person in the world to be lonely would be me."

SHE'S A LITTLE BIT COUNTRY...

With almost all the Osmonds reaping the rewards of the teenybopper phenomenon, by late 1972 Marie wanted a piece of the action too. After she scored a #1 country hit with a remake of Anita Bryant's "Paper Roses," she teamed up with Donny when nature came knocking on his vocal chords. When Donny went into the studio to record "I'm Leaving It All Up to You," he realized

that his voice wasn't what it used to be: Puberty had struck. Marie came to the rescue and recorded the high parts on the song, and promptly sent it to #4. She wound up singing on the rest of the album, and that's when their acts merged, though they still continued with their solo careers.

While the duo were out promoting their hit song, they were noticed by Fred Silverman, then programming chief for ABC-TV. He lassoed them in to the channel and formed their weekly variety show, *Donny & Marie*. The show was one part musical, one part comedy, one inexplicable part ice-skaters, and all parts Osmond. The whole family got in on the act. Donny became known for his purple socks and pratfalls. "I was always the fall guy, as they say, and I kind of ended up with a little bit of a stupid image," he says. Adds Marie, "It left kind of a stigma on him. You know, this Donny-goofy-silly kid."

Like everything else Donny and the Osmonds touched, the show turned to gold. It enjoyed a few successful years, but by the end of the '70s, Donny and Marie were on the verge of adulthood, and, however irrational, it didn't sit well with their fans. "All the little teenagers were now in their eighteen- to nineteen-year old stages. It was difficult for them to accept Donny and Marie in a much, much more mature role," says Donny. By 1979, the show had come to an end, and Donny found himself at an impasse.

"After the *Donny & Marie* show was over, I think Donny might have felt that he didn't have the career that he should have," says producer Mike Curb.

"All the attention was given to Marie," Donny says. "You know, 'She's the next thing we're going to push. Donny, you know, you've had your time. You're a has-been.' And it hurt. It really, really hurt." Ouch.

Add to all that the fact that Donny wanted to marry Debbie, his sweetheart of three years. (This was a young woman, he later found out, who "had a poster of me on her wall...She had David Cassidy, too. David Cassidy was on the front of the door, I was on the back of the door, go figure.") Sure, his fans wanted him to be happy...but, in their fantasies, his happiness directly involved them. Donny's mother, Olive, remembers the eventual fallout: "We were booked at Madison Square Garden for two nights. Sold out. And that morning it was announced that he was engaged to Debbie and half of them canceled their tickets. They sent back their fan club memberships in protest that they didn't want him to get married."

Regardless, Donny and Debbie took the plunge on May 8, 1977, and had to face the music. "My career went down the tubes. Because this teeny-

bopper eligible bachelor was now taken and I had to start over."

Donny found himself, at twenty, suddenly cast aside. "I couldn't figure out for the life of me how somebody could be so popular one day and then completely unpopular and uncool the next. Now, granted, I never had the guys. Guys always hated me. It was always a female following by and large. But even the females turned on me at a point in time because they grew up and said, 'Well, that's child stuff.' You know, that 'Puppy Love' stuff, that's for the kids....I did it too. It's a natural tendency to put away childish things. And I was a big part of people's childhood."

He refers to this time in his life as the lost years. "Because I was really lost, professionally. I wanted to change and the more they didn't let me change, the more I rebelled against that image."

LITTLE DONNY JONES

"When I ended *Donny & Marie* in '79, '80," Donny says, "there was still a demand out there for Osmond shows... but I could see way down the road that was eventually going to peter out, because people grow up, people lose interest, and we're playing smaller places, and I realize that something's gotta change."

With the Osmond brothers now country crooners, and Marie enjoying success on her own, Donny decided to leave the shackles of teen idoldom behind and try his luck on the Great White Way. He headed over to Broadway in 1982 to play the lead in a revival of George M. Cohan's *Little Johnny Jones.* (Coincidentally, David Cassidy starred in the West Coast version of the play.) The show met with scathing reviews, forcing it to close on the opening night. It was the first time Donny had failed at anything in his twenty-year career.

Donny needed a new plan—and a new image. People still saw him as the Donny who sang "Lollipops, Lace and Lipstick," or the Donny who hosted a family-friendly variety hour with his kid sister. The Donny who girls dreamt about. The Donny-cap-wearing Donny.

He says, "I had to, in a way, wake up the industry and say, you know what? I'm not that little kid that sang 'Puppy Love.' And I want everybody to know that I'm not putting 'Puppy Love' down, it was a great time in my life. But there comes a time when you want to change, you want to grow up, and you want to do something new and different."

Donny hired publicist Norman Winter to help him make the transition to a twenty-something rock star—not an easy task. "He was Mr. Nice Guy, that was the problem. He had the ability, but he didn't have the credibility," says Winter.

Finally, in 1986, Donny's luck turned around. By chance, he met Peter Gabriel at a UNICEF event, and Gabriel professed that he'd been an admirer. Gabriel invited him to come over to his studio in England and record some demos. It was all Donny needed to get back on track. "Peter Gabriel turned the perception of me, my life, around," he says.

Over in the U.K., Gabriel put in some good words at Virgin Records and Donny found himself with a contract to record songs for U.K. release. He was doing what he loved to do again, and with a newfound confidence. But the #1 hit remained elusive, though not for lack of trying.

"You do everything you can to get a record played," Donny says. "You just go to every party, you're just basically...kissing butt to everyone to get your record played. And then I realized I did too much when this magazine came out in England. It's like our *People* magazine here. It says what's happened this week. I was in every picture. They were just rubbing it in my face, rubbing it in Virgin's face, like, 'Man, you are trying way too hard.' Places I didn't even go, they superimposed me. It was the joke of England." Even though his single, "Soldier of Love," broke the U.K. Top 30, Virgin dropped Donny.

Just when he seemed ready to throw in the towel, a strange thing happened. Someone at New York City radio station WPLJ got his hands on "Soldier of Love."

They played the track and credited a "mystery artist," without revealing that Donny was behind it. He says they "were afraid of the image too, but they liked the music. And they did me a big favor by not saying it was me. And the lights lit up and [listeners] said 'We love this song.' It was the number-one requested song in New York, number-one market in the world. This is a dream come true. And every station across the country did the same thing, the mystery artist, and I did have them flying all over the place."

Once Donny fessed up, fans had the opposite reaction that he'd predicted—they welcomed him and the song with open arms, and sent the single to #2 on the U.S. charts. "Finally, finally, I was vindicated," Donny says.

Since then, Donny's career has enjoyed a second wind. In 1991, he returned to the theater in the title role in a touring production of *Joseph and the Amazing Technicolor Dreamcoat*. What was supposed to be a six-month tour of duty lasted six years. He and Marie premiered their second act on television in 1998 with a daytime talk show, which ran for two years. And more recently, he released a collection of pop-based Broadway show tunes called *This Is the Moment*. It may be a moment, but if it's anything like the rest of his career, it's sure to last. ✿

> ## "I don't know why the Osmonds always were looked down upon by the hard-core critics. Maybe I can to a certain extent, because I listen to some of the music that we came up with, and it was bubblegum—let's call it the way it was. 'Sweet and Innocent,' my first record, was exactly what the title said, sweet and innocent. But I don't think they ever gave the Osmond band credit for the kind of music that they were doing back in the early '70s."
>
> —DONNY

CHAPTER 5

RICK

(We All Need) The Aussie Touch

essie is a friend. It's hard to think of Rick Springfield without hearing those words—the opening line of the sexy pop confessional that anyone who came of age in 1981 can call up from memory in an instant. You think of Rick and you also remember the dashing Dr. Noah Drake from TV's *General Hospital,* saving lives and looking pretty. And you remember him running from mobs of screaming women in his movie *Hard to Hold.* (You *do* remember that, don't you?) Mostly you remember Rick Springfield as one of the reigning teen idols during the early '80s, sought after and adored, that guy who warned "Don't Talk to Strangers" and urged that "We all need the human touch..."

In the spring of 1981, it seemed as though Rick had arrived overnight to steal countless thumping hearts with his matinee-idol good looks, gritty pop tunes, and soap-star appeal. But what appeared to be instant success was actually the result of years of slowly and steadily—but never quietly—building the career that delivered him there. The son of an Australian army colonel, Rick moved around England and his homeland as a child, but nothing could have predicted the journey he would make as a rock star, a sometime actor, and two-time teen idol.

His real name is Richard Lewis Spring-thorpe, and he was born August 23, 1949, in Sydney, Australia. Both of young Rick's parents were passionate about music, and they passed that love onto him. Rick took up the guitar at thirteen—a five-dollar model procured from the local Woolworth's—and within months he and a friend were

SPRINGFIELD

"When we tried to move him away from that teenage image, the public just wouldn't buy it. He couldn't possibly be a rock star and have a face like he did."
—ROBIE PORTER, FORMER MANAGER

putting on shows in the family living room. At fifteen, he got his first electric guitar. Prone to depression from an early age, Rick admits that at that point in his life, "music saved me."

Rick joined a series of bands, among them the Jordy Boys, Wickedy Wak, and Rock House—a blues outfit. He dropped out of high school in tenth grade, and in November 1968, Rock House went on tour in Vietnam only to break up shortly after their return to Australia. His next band was Zoot, and by the time he joined forces with them, the band already had two hits, and were in "the throes of the whole pink teen thing," as Rick puts it. "Before I joined the band it was very teen pop, you know, pretty little guitar things. And when I joined them... I was trying to turn this little pop band into a heavy-metal band, which was pretty funny, actually. But the guys were all great musicians and everyone was very into it."

Zoot was wildly popular Down Under, most especially on the teen scene, and garnered an attention that was quite new to Rick. "I had never been very popular at school with girls, and I was always really just painfully shy," he says. "To have girls coming up to me at sixteen, seventeen, and eighteen, was like, 'What? I get this too?' Obviously pursuing music was really the heart of it. But the female attention was pretty fun."

Rick would also get his first taste of the hard work ahead of him, despite palpable chart success

and fan appreciation. "By the time we had four or five Top Ten singles, we were still making, like eighty bucks for a half-hour show. We used to haul our own gear, and we would do three shows a night, and it was just—for nothing. I mean, I had to live at home because I was making no money."

Soon Rick would say g'day to his Zoot mates and fly solo. He'd been noticed by producer Robie Porter while playing a show with Zoot. Rick says Porter "was interested in the band, but when the band looked like it wasn't going to work out, that we'd split up and didn't look like we were going to get back together again, he said 'why don't you make some solo songs?'... So I signed on with that, did one single, and it was a hit in Australia. And that got me a deal over here. Back then they were signing everybody in America. It was the '70s, so one single got me a deal." Porter joined forces with Steve Binder to become Rick's management team.

SKY'S THE LIMIT

In late 1971 at age twenty-two, Rick recorded his first solo single, "Speak to the Sky," and within a month of its release it had topped the Australian charts. It was all he needed to score a record deal at Capitol Records and a ticket to the States. When he got to Los Angeles in October 1972, the market for teen idols was wide open and raging, and Rick fit the bill completely. Gloria Staver at *16 Magazine* launched an all-out campaign to make him the next big teen dream. "All of a sudden," says Porter, "he was like the next David Cassidy, Donny Osmond—in that same era as they were."

Rick concedes, "It was a big ego stroke to arrive in the U.S. and suddenly your face is on all these magazines. It's hard not to be stroked by that." The immediate show of support seemed like it could only be a good thing. Rick, however, couldn't foresee the music industry bias that often goes with overwhelming teen adoration. "As far as I was concerned, at first I just thought it was publicity. I didn't differentiate between the teen publicity and adult publicity, radio publicity. I thought they were all the same."

Aptly titled *Beginnings,* Rick's debut album impressively shot up the Top 40 after only days in stores. What happened next might have felt like more of an ending for Rick. He was the victim of a nasty rumor that Capitol

had bused girls in to record stores to buy his album. After all, critics protested, how could a virtually unknown and unproven artist hit it so big so quickly? Capitol denied the charges, but radio DJs banned the album, and Rick's reputation was shattered. "Speak to the Sky," which had made it into the Top 20, would be his first and last hit off that album.

The whole ugly episode left Rick bewildered. He asked to be let out of his contract with Capitol and went over to Columbia Records. Within two years, he turned out his second solo album, *Comic Book Heroes,* but it was met with a steely reception from the radio industry, who'd doggedly held onto their tarnished image of Rick from the Capitol Records scandal. Without airplay, *Comic Book Heroes* would go nowhere, and Columbia washed its hands of Rick.

At that point, Rick says, "I didn't really know what I wanted, other than just to write songs. So there was a lot that I had to learn, and I think it was really unfortunate that things fell apart when they did. It was a tough, hard lesson, and it was a hard few years after that, really tough for me. But, in retrospect, it was a gift."

During that period, Rick's managers created *Mission: Magic!,* an animated TV show starring

Rick and his music, airing Saturday mornings on ABC. The weekly cartoon featured his likeness and voice, along with a new song written by Rick for each episode. The series ran for two seasons, but Rick found that he was fast becoming discontented with the direction his career was taking. He felt trapped by his teen-idol image, which was doing more to hurt his career than help it. "I was getting David Cassidy press, but I was writing songs about suicides and a guy leaving his wife and the kid," Rick says.

Says former manager Porter: "When we tried to move him away from that teenage image, the public just wouldn't buy it. He couldn't possibly be a rock star and have a face like he did." Ah, the eternal catch-22 of being a pop god.

In early 1975, Rick decided it was time to take stock of his situation. He'd just come out of a two-year relationship with *The Exorcist*'s head-turner Linda Blair (he describes it as "my first real full-on, just head-over-heels, almost adult relationship"). He desperately

needed to shed his teenybopper image; and he needed, finally, to make some money. At twenty-six years old, Rick found himself completely broke and depressed. He ditched his managers in an effort to make things right.

Rick went out and got himself a new management team: Tom Skeeter and Joe Gottfried. But this isn't the part in Rick's story where the clouds make way for the sun and everything starts looking up for our (comic book) hero. Says Skeeter, "We were turned down by every record company at least five times. And we just kept plugging and plugging and plugging." And plugging. Three years of pounding the pavement, playing in clubs, rebuilding a fan base, and recording demos would follow.

THE SECOND COMING OF RICK

Finally, in 1980, at age thirty-one, Rick landed a record deal with RCA. And this is where it gets good again. In February of the next year, he traded in his electric guitar for a stethoscope and joined the cast of *General Hospital* as Dr. Noah Drake. Shortly after his daytime debut, RCA released *Working Class Dog,* and Rick found himself, once again, thrust into the spotlight. Rick recalls: "It was suddenly, *Bang!* Full-throttle, all the way down, from 'I didn't put my seatbelt on yet.' It wasn't that, 'Wow, I can't believe this is happening.' It was, 'It's about freakin' time!'"

But in the middle of Rick's rocket ride to fame, his father died in Australia—an event that left Rick reeling. Colonel Springthorpe's encouragement and support through Rick's lean years, along with his shared love of music, had kept the two close across the miles. Rick would feel the loss for years to come; but now, there was little time to mourn. Rick's imminent climb to #1 would wait for nothing.

In August 1981, "Jessie's Girl" went to the top of the charts, and now he was everywhere. You could find him on TV, you could hear him on the radio, and you could see him on the covers of teen magazines. That's right—thirty-two years old and the guy was on the covers of teen glossies. "I had nothing to do with that," Rick says. "I mean, I didn't do any interviews or anything. It was just [that] they pulled out old stuff. ... So I had to defend myself as an honest musician and not some cute guy that had gotten lucky on a show and said, 'Hey, maybe I'll sing now.'"

Working Class Dog worked the charts. "I've Done Everything for You," penned by Sammy Hagar, went to #8, and "Love Is Alright Tonite," hit #20 shortly thereafter. In February 1982, Rick claimed a Grammy Award for Best Male Rock Vocal on "Jessie's Girl," which is, to this day, his most recognizable hit. The award was yet another milestone in Rick's constantly evolving career; a triumphant way of getting the world to take its eyes off his face for once and just listen.

Rick's follow-up album, *Success Hasn't Spoiled Me Yet,* appeared on the scene in 1982. Off that came "Don't Talk to Strangers," which grabbed hold of the #2 spot on the Top Ten; "What Kind of Fool Am I" and "I Get Excited" made a lot of noise on the charts as well.

Though *General Hospital* had taken good care of Rick, it was time for him to put all of his energy into his music, and Rick checked out. After all, he couldn't afford to fool around with his rock-star cred. The soap, he says, "didn't hurt record sales, but it sure hurt credibility which, in the end, is neither here nor there, I think. My goal has always been to write songs and have people enjoy them. Certain radio stations would drop the song when they found out I was on a soap opera and things like that. And in the end, I was only on the soap opera for eighteen months."

WIZARD OF OZ

His scrubs well behind him, Rick rocked the charts with his next album, *Living in Oz,* his 1983 platinum smash hit. Two tunes—"Affair of the Heart" and "Human Touch"—

grabbed hold of the Top 20. And then came *Hard to Hold.*

With Rick's chart success came a flood of movie offers. Rick, guided by his rock-star ego, chose the part with the most lines, the movie in which he'd be the lead. And that was *Hard to Hold.* Unfortunately for Rick, most critics found it hard to watch. The movie was a flop, and for all of his efforts to convince critics that he was a serious musician, the picture derailed him. The soundtrack, however, was another story. "Love Somebody" went to #5 on the pop charts, and the singles "Don't Walk Away" and "Bop 'Til You Drop" also made a pretty respectable showing in the Top 30. But, ultimately, the flick did its damage.

"I think it hurt my career overall," says Rick. "I remember a lot of people considered ["Love Somebody"] a real breakthrough song for me—writing-wise. They thought it was a tougher kind of sounding song. But I think the movie wasn't very compatible with what the music was saying. Where the music was going. And it was a light love story and I think a lot of the fans really liked it because it fed into that, but it didn't make any new fans. People were looking for me to make a next step, and that wasn't it."

The next few years were a series of highs and lows for Rick. He got married to Barbara Porter in 1984 and shortly after the two became parents. His 1985 effort *Tao* didn't meet with the same level of success as his last few outings, but it spawned two Top 30 singles. Rick found himself battling a depression that never really seemed to disappear. It was time to take a leave of absence from music and try to fix things from the inside out.

When he reemerged three years later, it was with *Rock of Life,* an album he planned to support with a massive tour. The night before the start of the tour, however, Rick was in an accident while riding his 4-wheel all-terrain vehicle. His collarbone was shattered and six ribs were broken in the collision. Prevented from touring, with a record he couldn't promote, Rick slid once again into depression.

After a year's worth of introspection, Rick came to the conclusion that he'd take an extended break from music and focus his energy on being a house-dad. When asked what's been the best time in his life, Rick unequivocally answers, "It has to be my kids. That's what comes to mind is my kids and the life of my kids. I can't think of anything that pleases me more. That's the only joy I think I've had that's totally non–ego based. So it's really pure."

Ten Rick-less years passed. He went from teen idol to family man, and he liked it that way. But he'd return to music—first with some live shows to feel things out, and then with an album in 1998. Call it *Karma.* Literally. Rick released *Karma* and toured on its behalf. In 2001, fans found Rick on the Vegas strip starring in *EFX Alive*, doing what he does best.

No doubt fans are getting their money's worth from the former teen dream, though the reward, it seems, is all Rick's. "It's almost like I'm watching the audience now, whereas before I was watching me being watched by the audience. I enjoy it way more—it's like the difference of walking into a party and worrying how you look as opposed to walking into a party and checking everybody out and seeing what everybody's about." Clearly, the party ain't over yet. ✿

THE MEN OF DAYTIME TV

Enough pop pinups have made the rounds in the hallowed halls of *General Hospital* that you have to wonder: Was it just a coincidence or was some kind of music bug going around? Whether they played doctors, orderlies, or regular citizens of the long-running soap, one thing was certain—they were all pulling double shifts.

Shaun Cassidy

CHARACTER: Dusty Walker
ON AIR: 1987
BUBBLEGUM DAYS:
Shaun became a hit with the girls a decade before checking into *GH*, with his #1 single, "Da Do Ron Ron."

Ricky Martin

CHARACTER: Miguel Morez
ON AIR: 1994-95
POP CONNECTION:
Ricky was in between his second and third albums (*Me Amaras* and *A Medio Vivir* when he appeared in Port Charles as a long-haired, studly bartender with a big secret. Turned out Miguel was a huge pop sensation in his homeland.

Rick Springfield

CHARACTER: Dr. Noah Drake
ON AIR: 1981-83
BREAKTHROUGH SINGLE:
"Jessie's Girl" was climbing the charts just as Dr. Drake was establishing his residency on the show.

John Stamos

CHARACTER:
Blackie Parrish
ON AIR: 1982-84
GOT MUSICAL:
John played with the Beach Boys on "Kokomo," among other songs, long after his poster-boy days.

Jack Wagner

CHARACTER: Frisco Jones
ON AIR: 1983-88:
1989-91: 1994-95
HIT SINGLE:
"All I Need." He also released *Don't Give Up Your Day Job,* which, thankfully, he didn't.

... and don't forget:

Michael Damian

CHARACTER: Danny Romalotti on *The Young and the Restless*
ON AIR: 1981-98
HIT SINGLE: The 1989 chart-topper, "Rock On." Apparently, he, too, followed Jack Wagner's advice.

CHAPTER 6

LEIF

"The worst thing about that time period? It would be the girls. The best thing? The girls."
—LEIF

California Dreamy

GARRETT

Donny Osmond became a teen idol after spending years in the music business, at that age when boys start to notice girls and girls started to notice him. David Cassidy stumbled into it when he landed a TV role and the show's producers realized they had a marketable hottie on their hands. Both stars were big business—hot commodities that could sell virtually anything with their photos on it, from magazines to lunch boxes. So it comes as no surprise that record producers would latch onto this phenomenon, use it as a business model, and try to reproduce it: find the right face at the right age, someone who can sing, dance, and make girls go ga-ga. A manufactured teen idol. Leif Garrett fit the mold.

Leif got his start in show business as a child actor. He made his film debut in 1969's *Bob and Carol and Ted and Alice,* and from there he made the rounds on television. A starring role in the short-lived series *Three for the Road* at age fourteen propelled his face onto the covers of the teen magazines. Letters from love-starved teenagers came pouring in by the thousands. After all, those curly blond locks and surfer-boy good looks were hard to resist.

It was all Leif needed to get a record deal. It was as easy, he says, as getting a call from a management team that went something like this: "'Hey kid, you want to make a record?' [I said] 'Yeah. Of course. I love music.'"

Says former manager Stan Moress: "I first heard about Leif with my two partners, Tony and Ben Scotti. Someone [from CBS

television] had called us about this kid. He was all over the teenage magazines and he was getting five to ten thousand letters a week. Somebody said, 'Can he sing?' And they said, 'Yeah, he can sing.' So Tony Scotti and I immediately tracked him down, brought him in for a meeting, and we thought the kid was magic. So we signed him for management, and then Tony actually went and made a deal with Atlantic Records, and I believe it was their very first teenage artist—teen idol—that they had ever signed."

The song didn't get a whole lot of radio airplay, but it did score him a record contract. In 1977, Leif signed an exclusive five-album deal with Scotti Brothers. He briefly recorded first on Atlantic Records, and then when the Scottis established their own label, Leif moved over there. That same year, Leif announced his arrival with the appropriately titled *Leif Garrett,* which generated his first Top 20 hit, a teenybopper remake of "Surfin' U.S.A." The response was encouraging enough to send little Leif out on tour. And

> ## "When Leif would come on stage he would carry himself out there in spandex and golden hair. Girls would faint. He was adored like a god."
> —DON CUGINI

And so a pubescent star was born. Well, almost. First he had to get the singing thing down. Producer Michael Lloyd, who knew the Scottis from his days at MGM Records, remembers that "Leif was excited about trying. And to his credit, he gave it everything he had. We needed another year or two of development for his voice. For him to feel comfortable in the studio. And little by little, he started to get more comfortable and more confident."

Lucky for Leif, Lloyd was already in the teen-idol business. Having worked with Shaun Cassidy and the Osmonds, he knew the musical formula for pop-star success and hand-picked the songs Leif would sing. "First time we went to record a song called 'Come Back When You Grow Up'... he gave it everything he had," Lloyd says. "Leif was tireless, he was always eager to do better, he wanted to learn and he wanted to be successful."

that's when the madness really kicked in. Says Leif, "As soon as the first single came out, it was over. There was no turning back. It was huge."

HE WAS MADE FOR DANCING

On tour for the first time, Leif fashioned himself after more established rock 'n' rollers. "I was definitely a big Rod Stewart, Elton John, Led Zeppelin fan. Those were the bands I dug," he says; when he would strut his stuff on stage, it was a tribute to the virility of someone like Mick Jagger. His management, on the other hand, went after the saccharine factor, having created a highly marketable teen dream machine. Moress admits that their "goal all along was to make him an international star.

"He caught on almost immediately from the first release because he already had a fan base," says Moress. "All we had to do was market the fan base and expand the fan base and he was in every teen magazine, he was on television, he was in the newspapers, he was everywhere. It became a snowball effect. The harder he wanted to work, the more we wanted to work. And, I must say, Leif did work hard. He did go all over the world and it was quite exhausting at times and he had his moments. But for the most part he was a good promotional partner." Leif posters, Leif T-shirts, Leif magazines, Leif fan club memberships. All the teenage world wanted—and could buy—a piece of Leif.

What seemed like a sure thing to his

LOVE 'EM AND LEIF 'EM

"When I entered the Leif's Kisses [contest], I had no idea that I would win. I had never won anything in my life. Then I saw my name in Tiger Beat and the city I was from—I really did win. I received the Kisses and glass jar they came in and boy, was I excited. Then that same year, Leif's concert came to Busch Gardens in Williamsburg, my hometown. I took the jar of Kisses to the concert to try and get backstage to meet Leif. My cousin's mother tried to explain everything to an event staffer about me winning the contest. We never did get backstage and I was so devastated and mad, too. As a thirteen-year-old, I was traumatized."

—PATTY, THIRTY-EIGHT

49

"We had three to five thousand girls surrounding a building. I was scared to death. We had to take him around in an armored car." —STAN MORESS

managers came as something of a surprise to Leif. "The last thing I expected was the adulation to happen so quickly and so drastically. I mean, it was worldwide overnight," he says. He immediately became a hot commodity overseas. Record store appearances nearly turned into riots, full of girls vying to get a glimpse of the bushy-haired babe. Guitarist Don Cugini remembers shows where "Leif came onto the stage and children collapsed unconscious."

On the recording front, the hyperventilating young honeys were treated to juiced-up oldies, à la Leif. While the other teen idols were out there chewing on their bubblegum hits, Leif's debut album featured remakes like "Put Your Head on My Shoulder" and "The Wanderer." His songs were cherry-picked by Ben and Tony Scotti. Together, says Moress, they "had a real good song sense, because they had worked with the Osmonds; they had worked with David Cassidy. They had worked with all these teen idols. And they had a real sense of the marriage between what they felt the public would buy and what they felt he could sing." Instinct paid off, sending Leif's next single, "Runaround Sue," to #13 on the charts, extending his tenure as a teen idol.

"My best friend as a kid, Linda, used to play Leif's records constantly and make up dances to his songs. I can still remember the dance we made up to 'I Was Made for Dancin'."
—JULIE, THIRTY-THREE

"Leif brought my best friend and I back together somehow. After years apart, when I turned fourteen, Debbie and I ran into one another and started raving about this cute singer we were in love with—just to find out it was the same guy...Leif. That was wonderful. From then on, we were inseparable again."
—JANIE, THIRTY-SEVEN

Despite their expertise, Leif felt as though his management may have been missing the mark when it came to what kids really wanted, musically speaking. Though he describes the crest of Leif-mania as "an endless wave," he goes on to say that "It was very much like the song not ending. For me, it was definitely that the song was a little too long, because I wanted to change in the middle of everything. There was a lot of me that wanted to grab the bull by the horns and say, 'Hey, look, I'm of the age of the people who are buying my records, and this is what we're at, where I'm

The girls were as wild about him as ever. Leif was occupying prime real estate in the teen magazines. Fans loved to read about him and his fantastic rock star life—whether it was true or not was irrelevant. It was the fantasy that had them at hello. Says Leif, "Even if there was some truth to some of the articles, it was never just reality. They would always embellish. Part of that persona of my image being so squeaky clean was kept up by teen magazines. Weird stuff, like 'What Leif dreams about at night.' They'd make up stuff. Who knew what I dreamt about? I never told anybody what I dreamt about, it was nobody's business. The last thing I was going to do was let people in on what I was dreaming about."

at. I know the people who are listening to my music are not unlike myself.'... And it just didn't happen that way. It had very much the teen idol syndrome of, 'This is what works. We stick with it, kid.'"

"I wanted to be making the records. I wanted to be going on tour. I wanted to be living that life. But not in that what I considered a lesser rock 'n' roll vein—the pop vein." —LEIF

Still, that "if it ain't broke, don't fix it" approach gave Leif his first Top Ten single on both sides of the ocean in 1978. The song was "I Was Made for Dancin'"—off his second album, *Feel the Need*—a surefire hit with the young ladies. "When I heard it," Leif says, "I didn't think it was going to be such the hit that it was. It was a lot more lightweight than what I wanted to be doing. But it had kind of a hook to it. I liked the verses better than I liked the chorus. It was the perfect timing. 'I Was Made for Dancing' was in the height of disco and it was a catchy little ditty."

The adoration, in retrospect, was hard for Leif to buy. "After a while, you start thinking, 'God, what are they after?' Well, they're after an ideal. They're after a perfect scenario that goes on in their head. For someone who's telling me, back then, 'Oh my God, Leif, I love you.' How could they possibly love me? How could somebody possibly love me? They don't know me. They know what they read, and they see what they see, they hear what they hear. All those things put together, they might be in love with that. But they don't really know Leif Garrett, and especially back then they didn't really know Leif Garrett."

So who *was* the real Leif Garrett? By then Leif was already partaking in the seedier side of the music business. "Right away, I dove right in the rock 'n' roll world. That all started really young, like fourteen," he says. Among his vices were drinking, marijuana, and cocaine. What's more is that the private Leif was already spoken for. Since age fifteen, he'd been in a relationship with actress Nicolette Sheridan, who lived with Leif, his mother, and sister. But none of this extracurricular behavior was appropriate fodder for the teen glossies, so fans stayed blissfully ignorant.

FEEL THE NEED TO ROCK OUT

In 1979, Leif released his third album, *Same Goes for You,* and headed out on a nine-week, thirty-seven-city tour of the States. Being on the road, away from his managers, gave him the freedom to rock out onstage to covers of his favorite artists. Says guitarist Cugini, "Leif had to be who he was. Leif couldn't be dancing on a birthday cake for the rest of his life. He was a guy, a guy onstage singing nursery rhymes, and he didn't like it. He wanted to play rock. So rock we did."

Offstage, Leif continued to indulge his rock star lifestyle, which only led him into trouble. Five days short of his eighteenth birthday, Leif and his friend Roland Winkler were at a party and, having had a few too many, went on a drug run. Leif was driving. One wrong turn of the wheel on the Hollywood Freeway sent the car flying down an eighty-foot embankment. Roland was left paralyzed from the waist down. It was an accident that would haunt Leif for years to come.

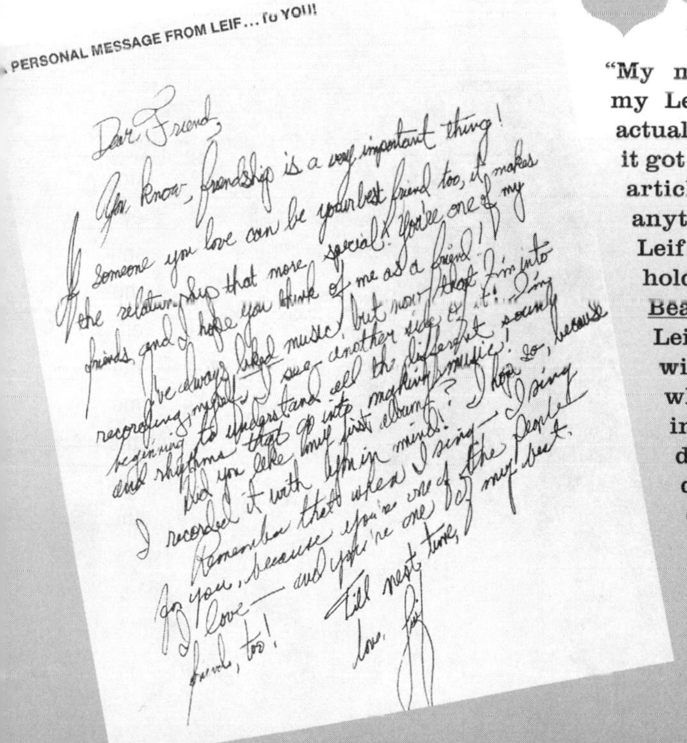
A PERSONAL MESSAGE FROM LEIF . . . to YOU!

Dear Friend,

You know, friendship is a very important thing! If someone you love can be your best friend too, it makes the relationship that more special! You're one of my friends, and I hope you think of me as a friend!

I've always liked music, but now that I'm into recording myself, I see another side of it! I'm beginning to understand all the different sounds and rhythms that go into making music!

Did you like my first album? I hope so, because I recorded it with you in mind! Remember that when I sing—I sing for you, because you're one of the people I love—and you're one of my best friends, too!

Till next time,

Love, Leif

"My most prized possession is my Leif Garrett scrapbook. It's actually three scrapbooks because it got to be so big. It contains Leif articles, pictures, clippings—anything that I could find on Leif. It has pockets in it that hold fan club newsletters, *Tiger Beat* Leif books, and other Leif tidbits. I would never part with it....As a teen, anyone who knew of me knew I was into Leif big-time. I wore a different Leif button every day. My locker was Leif-decorated inside. A few people left me Leif in their [high school yearbook] 'senior wills.'"

—DOPHINE, THIRTY-EIGHT

The following year, Leif jetted off to Florida to complete *Can't Explain,* the fourth album under his contract with Scotti Brothers. Away from his managers, he seized the opportunity to break out of the teenybopper tunes and record *his* kind of music. "I came back into town thinking that this is going to be my breakthrough crossover that was going to allow people to see me in a different light from being a quote-unquote clean-cut teen idol, as opposed to the rebellious head that I was," he says. But according to Leif, the Scottis weren't having it. At their insistence, Leif recorded what would be the first single from the album, "Had to Go and Change on Me."

So much for self-expression. "More than anything, what really had disillusioned me came after I finished the fourth record. I realized that there was no way that they were going to allow me any creative input into how we were going to change musically. They wanted to keep the formula: 'This is what works, kid. We made you, you're nothing without us.'"

The album was a flop. And it seemed as though Leif's fans were off finding new pop princes to pin their dreams on. He'd had a good run as a teen idol, but just as he was growing up, so were his fans. Says Moress, "I think the public is fickle and I think that when they've had enough—and they certainly got saturated with Leif—they move on. It's like in any genre of music, you move on, and particularly with teen idols. The next star would come along and they'd gravitate to that star."

Lloyd attributes Leif's diminishing popularity to the changing face of radio in 1980. "AM radio was slowly losing its fan base and FM radio was becoming more popular in terms of pop records. FM had been more progressive music. Now FM was starting to become pop oriented. And I think radio was searching for audiences—the pop stations started to lose their support."

Leif still had one more album to finish out his contract. *My Movie of You* was released in 1981, and Leif was finally glad to be done with that phase of his career. After that, he says, "I didn't really go anywhere. Basically, I went underground. I just wanted to have time to be alone, be away from all the controlling factors. Plus, I knew then that the only thing that would ever allow me to break free from the teen idol image—because it was such a strong image— would be time. And, oddly enough, people still sometimes think of me as a long-blond-haired, skateboarding, surfing sixteen-year-old."

Perhaps that's because even today, there are still legions of fans with a special place in their thirtysomething hearts for Leif. A quick surf of the Web shows that some loyalties never die. And to that end, neither do teen idol memorabilia collections. Leif, in all his curly-blond grandeur, occupies many a bedroom wall to this day. To many of those who held him near and dear to their hearts, Leif Garrett is still really big business. ❧

CHAPTER 7

Shadow Dancer

"That was when he was at his best. At that age, wanting to be successful, not having the success, but having the hunger. The music was everything."
—BARRY GIBB

When it's 1967 and your older brothers are the Bee Gees and they've got four Top 20 hits with no sign of success stopping anytime soon, you want to be a singer too. So, when you're thirteen, your oldest brother, Barry, buys you a guitar; and when you're sixteen, that same older brother, looking out for you, introduces you to the guy who launched the Bee Gees' career. Now it's your turn to have a go at topping the charts, touring the world, and making teenage girls weak in the knees at the sound of your voice. You're Andy Gibb, of course—the Aussie music sensation who hit it very big, very fast.

For two years after meeting Robert Stigwood, founder of RSO Records, Andy honed his act in the bars and clubs of his homeland. Says Stigwood, "I'd seen him perform in Australia and I thought he was sensational." So, in 1976, when Andy turned eighteen, Stigwood summoned him and his young bride, Kim (née Reeder), over to the States to work on his first album.

In 1977, only six months after stepping foot on American soil, Andy released *Flowing Rivers*, a disco-influenced debut that would yield two #1 singles. "I Just Want to Be Your Everything"—written and produced by big brother Barry—was first in rotation; its follow-up, "(Love Is) Thicker Than Water," knocked his brothers' "Stayin' Alive" out of the top position. Two weeks later, the Bee Gees stole the spot back from their little brother with "Night Fever."

Immediately, Andy became a big hit with the high school set. His face graced the covers of countless teen magazines, with such typical headlines as ANDY GIBB CONFESSES: WHY I'M AFRAID OF GIRLS and LOVE IS...with a picture of the shirtless young stud. Kim, his wife at the time, says, "He was on the front of all those teenybopper magazines and I suppose they had to give the perception that he was available." And so they did.

The overwhelming attention and the super-quick rise to fame proved to be a challenge for nineteen-year-old Andy. "I think he must have had it in his mind what it was going to be like. But I don't think he knew how to deal with it once it happened," says Barry. Andy was indulging in the seedier

GIBB AND TAKE

In 1978, the airwaves were dominated by the brothers Gibb. Between Andy's sizzling solo career and the Bee Gees' Saturday Night Fever soundtrack, there was enough falsetto on the charts to make the Four Seasons proud. And that same year, "Grease" was the word—thanks to big brother Barry, who wrote the title track for Frankie Valli and it also went to #1. Coincidentally, both blockbusters featured fledgling teen idol John Travolta. Talk about synergy.

TOP 5, FEBRUARY 4, 1978
1. "Stayin' Alive," Bee Gees
2. "Short People," Randy Newman
3. "Baby Come Back," Player
4. "We Are the Champions," Queen
5. "(Love Is) Thicker Than Water," Andy Gibb

TOP 5, MARCH 11, 1978
1. "(Love Is) Thicker Than Water," Andy Gibb
2. "Night Fever," Bee Gees
3. "Sometimes When We Touch," Dan Hill
4. "Emotion," Samantha Sang (written by Barry and Robin Gibb)
5. "Lay Down Sally," Eric Clapton

TOP 5, MARCH 18, 1978
1. "Night Fever," Bee Gees
2. "Stayin' Alive," Bee Gees
3. "Emotion," Samantha Sang
4. "Lay Down Sally," Eric Clapton
5. "(Love Is) Thicker Than Water," Andy Gibb

MAY 13, 1978
1. "If I Can't Have You," Yvonne Elliman (written by Barry, Maurice, and Robin Gibb)

TOP 5, JUNE 17, 1978
1. "Shadow Dancing," Andy Gibb
2. "You're the One That I Want," John Travolta and Olivia Newton-John
3. "Baker Street," Gerry Rafferty
4. "It's a Heartache," Bonnie Tyler
5. "Too Much, Too Little, Too Late," Johnny Mathis and Deniece Williams

"When he was under the influence, that wasn't him at all. It was somebody else who took over." —BARBARA GIBB

side of the business and it was ruining his relationships one by one, including his marriage. Kim was usually left behind while Andy partied and toured...and partied some more.

Andy's mother, Barbara Gibb, says, "When he was under the influence, that wasn't him at all. It was somebody else who took over..But the next day he'd be back apologizing to everybody. He didn't know what he'd done, but he'd be sorry."

Barry, Maurice, and Robin attributed Andy's behavior to what they called "first fame." Barry explains: "First fame is a very dangerous thing. You believe what you read about yourself, you believe what people say about you. You believe that you have something very special to say and that God's talking through you. This happens to you when you become famous for the first time. Especially at an international level. So I think it was a little crazy for him for a while."

So crazy that he wound up hurting his marriage for good. Pregnant a year into the marriage, Kim gave her husband an ultimatum: me or the drugs. Andy kept on with his reckless ways, and his wife went back to her old life in Australia, where she gave birth to their daughter.

Andy's second album, *Shadow Dancing*, was unveiled in the summer of 1978. He claimed another #1 hit with the title song off that album, and accomplished what no other artist had ever done before: his first three singles had all gone to #1. At this point, Andy had moved

to Miami to be closer to his brothers, and he briefly dated goody-goody Marie Osmond. (Let's just say they made beautiful music together.) He also had two more big hits off *Shadow Dancing:* "An Everlasting Love" and "(Our Love) Don't Throw It All Away." Both made it into the Top Ten.

Still, the drugs and alcohol were sending his life into a tailspin. He was spending more money than he had and running up a huge debt. His brothers suspected cocaine was to blame for his erratic behavior, and when they tried to intervene, Andy fled. He relocated to Malibu, and tried to make it on his own from there.

Don't Throw It All Away

Now on the West Coast, Andy tried to get back on top of his game. 1980 saw the release of his third effort, *After Dark*, as well as a greatest-hits LP. Despite the fact that the album garnered a #4 hit with "Desire" and a #12 single with "I Can't Help It" (sung with Aussie compatriot Olivia Newton-John), the album suffered when it came to sales. Poor record performance coupled with Andy's penchant for drugs left his label no choice but to drop him from its roster. Recalls Stigwood, "I tried and tried. And [it] absolutely broke my heart."

Andy didn't stray too far from music, though. He soon landed a job cohosting the hit television series *Solid Gold*. He split his time between taping the show and starring in the musical *Pirates of Penzance*, with Pam Dawber, the human half of TV's *Mork & Mindy*. In his personal life, his leading lady was *Dallas* star Victoria Principal, whom he met on *The John Davidson Show*.

Though it seemed like he'd finally gotten a few good things going, drugs continued to sabotage his success. By the summer of 1982, his erratic behavior—namely failing to show up for work—got him canned from both gigs. Principal, who described Andy as "simply the nicest person I've ever known," soon found herself in a similar situation as Andy's ex-wife Kim once did. "I asked him to either choose me or choose drugs," Principal

Amazing Technicolor Dreamcoat. Opening night was met with fantastic reviews; yet the following night, the people's Joseph called in sick. In fact, over the next six weeks, he'd call in sick twelve times—enough for the show's producers to send him packing.

By the time he was twenty-five, Andy had gone from playing to thousands of adoring fans to smoky Vegas nightclubs—the difference between night and day for the onetime teen idol. Over the next few years, he'd go on and off of cocaine binges, in and out of rehab, and rack up more than a million dollars in debt, forcing him to file for bankruptcy. Declaring financial ruin, says Barry, "was a dashing blow to Andy. I don't think he survived that. He was embarrassed by it."

Andy returned to Miami and the comfort of his brothers, who tried to resurrect his ailing career. They wrote and produced four new tracks for their little brother, which earned him a deal with Island Records in London. The label asked that he come over to England to work on more songs, and he quickly set up shop in his brother Robin's country estate.

Away from the protective unit of his older brothers, things sadly began to crumble one last time. Robin remembers: "I had to keep reassuring him of his talent and build up his confidence. It actually affected his mind that he had to really start again." Not only were his spirits deteriorating but so was his health. His body had been wracked by years of drug and alcohol abuse, and his heart was weak. On March 10, 1988, just five days after his thirtieth birthday, Andy died of heart failure. ✿

says. "And though I know with all his heart he wanted to choose me, he chose drugs." The two lovebirds broke up, leaving Andy alone and devastated.

HE AIN'T HEAVY, HE'S OUR LITTLE BROTHER

For a few short months, Andy was able to clean up his act and refrain from using drugs. Making it apparent once again that people were willing to give his talent a chance, Andy landed the lead role in the Broadway production of *Joseph and the*

CHAPTER 8

DURAN

"We used to get chased all over the place.
It would be like a scene from the Keystone Cops.
We'd be in one car and then there would
be photographers and other cars and
then there would be kids, and sometimes
it was just insane." —JOHN TAYLOR

Boys on Film

DURAN

They came together when punk was almost done beating its fists and disco was moving to its last beat. Not quite rock, not quite pop, and certainly not New Wave, Duran Duran formed in the late '70s with a reactionary sound. They were like nothing you'd ever heard before. Or seen. Five good-looking guys from Birmingham, England, who took some of their cues from glam rock and turned out a lusty brand of pop song you could dance to. Their timing was impeccable. At the start of the '80s, the music scene in England was about to explode into several different directions; in the States, music fans were about to get their first taste of Music Television. And all over the world, almost overnight, Duranies were born.

Duran Duran went through several lineup changes before they landed the stellar combination of Nick Rhodes, John Taylor, Andy Taylor, Simon LeBon, and Roger Taylor. The next four years, from '80 to '84, were, in John's words, "magic"— hit singles, breakthrough videos, phenomenal fame, world tours, teenage adoration, and, obviously, great music. Over the years, its members have changed—some departed, some new— and a reconfigured Duran Duran continues to make music today. But this is the story of what it was like to

be there at the height of their success, the heyday of their teen-idol reign, when it seemed that all the world wanted a piece of these five guys.

The group was formed by John Taylor and Nick Rhodes, childhood friends with a shared interest in glam rock. From their early teens, the boys' aspirations were clear cut. "We wanted to take rock music onto the dance floor. We wanted our sound to become one that everybody liked," says Nick. "From early on that was our dream. All we wanted to do was to get involved in the music business and to be in a band. The only problem was having to learn how to play an instrument, which came later."

Together with Simon Colley and Steven Duffy in 1978, they named themselves after a character in Jane Fonda's sci-fi flick, *Barbarella*. John played bass and Nick was on keyboards. Colley and Duffy wouldn't last beyond '79 though, and in the next year or so there was something of a revolving door of players. One that stayed on the inside was drummer Roger Taylor. Shortly after, an

ad for a guitarist in *Melody Maker* delivered Andy Taylor. "He brought practical knowledge that none of us had," says John. "We knew how to match lipgloss and eyeliner. But he knew how to change guitar strings."

The lads became the house band at the Rum Runner, a Birmingham dance club owned by brothers Paul and Michael Berrow, who had modeled the club after the then-thriving Studio 54 in New York. The Berrows, who'd never been in the music biz, were about to land their first big act. They became Duran Duran's managers in 1980, and put the boys to work. Literally. Michael Berrow recalls, "John and Roger used to collect glasses and wash up. Andy worked in the kitchen as a co-helping cook. Nick was the DJ... so everybody was pulling all of the stops out. It was a collective mission even then. The work ethic was strong. Everybody worked day and night, really. It was good fun."

With the three Taylors—no relation—and Nick, the group was still short a singer.

Enter Simon LeBon. "We thought we were never going to find a singer, actually," Nick says. "It had been a two-year process with all these lineup changes, and then a girl who worked at the Rum Runner said, 'Oh I know somebody you might like.'...At this stage we would have met anybody because we were desperate for a singer—we had so much material. He came down to one of our rehearsals one day...he looked right, and he had lyrics."

> "You had to get America. It's a funny old thing about the ambition of a British group. If you ask the ambition of a British group, ultimately America would be top of the list, to break America. If you broke Europe, you pay the bills. **If you broke America, you had a life.**"
>
> —ANDY TAYLOR

In 1980, Duran Duran began touring the U.K. and shook hands on a deal with the record label EMI. Essentially, not having a formula for success became the group's formula for success. "We'd never been in the music business before, so I think that was an advantage," Michael Berrow admits. "Not knowing any rules, we had no preconceptions about anything. So we made it up as we went along. And the more fun it was, the more confident we became that we found a very rich vein of entertainment."

Quickly, they built a following in the U.K., playing small venues while their first album, *Duran Duran,* climbed the charts. They also spent some time in the United States, playing the Roxy in Los Angeles and the Ritz in New York, a hotbed for just-through-Customs British acts, in 1981. Says Nick, "The audience was a real shock to us. Talk about a band that came from underground clubs and this sort of dark side of music, suddenly getting this hysteria, it was puzzling and something we just didn't understand."

VIDEOS MADE THEM RADIO STARS

Their first single, "Planet Earth," hit the #12 spot on the U.K. charts, while their eponymous debut album went to #3 with sales of more than 2.5 million. On their way to becoming the next fab fivesome, Duran Duran were able to cash in on their star-quality looks and high style in a new medium that was theirs for the taking: the music video. Russell Mulcahy, who directed many of their early videos, says, "They not only understood the importance of [music video], they actually sort of enjoyed doing it. They felt that they were doing something which was entertainment, and would be watched and enjoyed.... They had their musical stage, worked very hard on producing the great sound. But I think they worked just as hard on their videos, for what it was. It was a piece of cinema."

ISN'T IT ROMANTIC?

♥ ♥ ♥ ♥ ♥ ♥ ♥

Think back to the music coming out of Britain in the early '80s: Frankie Goes to Hollywood; Soft Cell; Kajagoogoo; Spandau Ballet; OMD. A softer, more danceable kind of rock music. Synthesizers and drum machines. Eyeliner and pretty clothes. Those were the New Romantics, and Duran Duran were its poster boys. Nile Rodgers, who produced a number of the group's hits, recalls: "In retrospect, I would say that Duran Duran had all of the elements for that whole New Romantic phase. They had the groove and the vibe. They definitely had the look. And they had the songs, they had the composition."

Inspired by the glam-rock ethic of David Bowie and the high style of Roxy Music, the New Romantics were a thoughtful and fashionable alternative in a postpunk era. As much as it was about music, it was also about style. "It's a big cliché now, men being in touch with the female side of themselves," says Simon LeBon. "It wasn't then. It really wasn't then. It was something really new, not to be macho and not to kind of base your whole ethic on being the strongest. But actually to base your ethic on being attractive and being clever, being smart."

By the mid-'80s the romance was fading. It's a shame they couldn't have kept rock's spandex years at bay just a little while longer.

It was a new way to gain exposure; or in the case of the "Girls on Film" clip, overexposure. The song went to #5 in the U.K., but its racy skinflick was banned on the BBC and the newly created MTV. Over the next few years, MTV would seem as though it had been created for a band like Duran Duran; their sexy mini-epics took place in such exotic lands as Sri Lanka and Antigua, the story lines were full of intrigue, great clothes, and beautiful women—just the kind of thing that made you want your MTV.

Duran Duran set out to conquer the States in 1983. Back home, their existence had sent teenage girls into a tizzy; Stateside, they were riding high on the pop charts, with "Hungry Like the Wolf" spinning into heavy rotation on MTV. During the same time, "Is There Something I Should Know" debuted at #1 in the U.K.—a feat just a privileged few (Elvis, the Beatles) have achieved. Duran mania wasn't just picking up momentum, it was an unstoppable beast.

Simon remembers, "When we got to America we did an in-store signing at the Video Shack in Times Square. Somebody said there were just a few people out there, but then we arrived—and there were four thousand people. They completely encircled the block. They had to call in twelve mounted police to come and do something with these people. We got in there and it was absolutely incredible. We must have been in there signing for two hours and there were still thousands of people who could have carried on.... We got back to the hotel that night, it was on the ABC news at six, and we thought, 'Gentlemen, we have arrived.'" Upon returning home, the band packed their bags and left industrial Birmingham for hip London.

Richard Blade, a DJ who'd become a friend of the band, recalls one of their first American press conferences, which he'd hosted in Hollywood, California. "It really was like Beatlemania. The security was intense. There were limos everywhere. And still somehow the fans had found out. Outside Magic Castle there were maybe ten to twenty thousand kids, and the limos had to get through this crowd. There was press from all over the world. I was sitting on the stage with these five guys from Duran Duran, thinking, *how on Earth are they going to keep their head?* Not only with the kids and fans screaming, but now here's these grown-up guys in the press who are screaming at them."

Simon knew the band had the right attitude. He says, in retrospect, "I think that the life of any band, or anybody who's suddenly thrust into the public eye and this incredible attention—it is bizarre. And I don't think anybody—well, people do start to take it seriously and I think that's when they get problems. We never did. Wo

always said it was part of the job. Yeah, there's four thousand people there and you've got to sign some autographs and they're all screaming for you and they want to see what's inside your trousers. You don't think *oh, wow, that makes me a really great person.* How wonderful. You just think, *oh well, that comes with the job.* That's what we're after. That means that people are listening to the music and those people are buying our records. That's great." Those records were being snatched up by the millions, while their singles—"Hungry Like the Wolf," "Rio," "Is There Something I Should Know," and "Union of the Snake"—tore up the charts at breakneck speed.

RAGGED TIGER BEAT

Duran Duran's third album, *Seven and the Ragged Tiger*—which spawned the singles "New Moon on Monday" and "The Reflex"—was devoured by fans in late 1983, selling one million copies the first month alone. The following

"We set ourselves aims and we said we're going to play Hammersmith Odeon by '82, Wembley by '83, and Madison Square Garden by '84. We were kind of methodical about it."

—JOHN TAYLOR

year, they set out on a major worldwide, whirlwind tour, giving young girls an opportunity to scream their hearts and lungs out for them. At the time, says DJ Richard Blade, "there was no other band like Duran Duran. Five great-looking guys that could play great music and could fit on the bedroom wall of every teenage girl in a poster."

large female audience the serious music critics didn't want to listen anymore. We were sort of blacklisted immediately, to the point of comedy in that people that had been writing great things about us just suddenly switched off to it. We've never had a great time with music critics. I think a lot of that's to do with the fact that they like bands that

"So *many* women

The adoration, Simon claims, was unexpected. "We suddenly found that we just had something that communicated with the young girls in the world. It was a real surprise to us. It never occurred to us that that would happen. We had an inkling because a lot of those magazines [like *Tiger Beat*] were very interested in doing shoots with us."

He also says, "I think a lot of the following for Duran Duran wasn't just about five good-looking young boys onstage waving it around. I think it was also that those songs spoke the language that people understood, when they were lying on their own in their bedrooms, there was a lot of teenage angst going down. You know—*My parents don't understand me but here's a song that really does communicate how I feel.* And I think that really worked for us."

The downside to such female adoration meant that critical success would be all the more elusive. Says Nick, "I think there's no question that because we developed a are for boys—and Duran Duran is for girls and boys and anything in between."

"We were the butts of some serious disrespect from the press," Simon says. "They said, I remember, 'they don't play their instruments.' They said we didn't even write our own songs. I think they thought we were like a completely contrived group that was just put together like the Monkees or something. And it was laughable. It was completely laughable."

Production guru Nile Rodgers, who worked with the band on *Notorious*, among other projects, explains: "Since they had like these little teenybopper fans, they wouldn't have a great deal of respect from the so-called

gave me their **underwear."**

—SIMON LeBON

establishment, or the hip music people. But frankly, they did good music. They did great songs....The unfortunate negative fallout of that process is the fact that whenever you have huge throngs of younger people digging your music, you lose a lot in the credibility factor."

Luckily, teenage girls madly in love care very little about credibility and record reviews. They proved their loyalty—and their lust—to the band night after night in concert. The group talks about this "wall of sound" at live shows like it's something out of mythology, the same mythology that worships pop idols.

"The screaming didn't stop," says John. "There's no recognition.... It was just a wall of hysteria."

Nick says, "It was getting really difficult with the live shows because we literally couldn't hear." Adds Simon, "When the screaming stopped, I suddenly realized how difficult it was to sing in tune, because for about a year before, I hadn't heard a single thing. I

71

FIGHT THE POWER STATION

Remember "Some Like It Hot" (...and some sweat when the heat is on...)? Or "Get It On" (...bang a gong, get it on)? Sure you do. That was Power Station. While Duran Duran was on hiatus in 1985, it divided into two different bands. Here's a rundown of what went down.

POWER STATION
Featuring John Taylor, Andy Taylor, Robert Palmer, and ex–Chic drummer Tony Thompson
   Albums: The Power Station, Living in Fear
   Songs you know you know: "Some Like It Hot"; "Get It On" (A retitled cover version of T. Rex's "Bang a Gong")
   Lineup changes: When Palmer departed, he was replaced by Michael Des Barres; later, when Taylor exited the Station, Bernie Edwards (ex–Chic) took his place.

ARCADIA
Featured Simon LeBon, Nick Rhodes, Roger Taylor
   Album: So Red the Rose
   Song you know you know: "Election Day"

was, obviously, in my mind singing one thing but what was actually coming out was probably something completely different.... The other thing about the screaming, of course, is if that's the kind of reaction you're getting, as far as the media's concerned, you must be a bag of shite, literally, because they're serious listeners. So we must be appealing to a different, baser instinct than love of music."

Audience hysteria is one thing. But everyday encounters with love-crazed fans proved more trying for the band—and more worrisome. Says Nick, "We went through an awful lot of crazy situations. My greatest fear about it was with the fans, that somebody was going to get very seriously hurt. Because when people reach that level of hysteria, they completely lose control of any sense of reality. And we were surrounded by this. I'd walk out of the backstage door or something, thinking that there was nobody there. And suddenly there would be five hundred people running at you."

REARVIEW TO A THRILL

By the end of 1984, still riding high on their wave of success, Duran Duran was ready for a break. They'd sold, by that point, five million albums; "The Wild Boys" had just peaked at #2; and the group released their live effort, *Arena*. But back home after an eighteen-month world tour, they decided to take an open-ended hiatus—which isn't to say they rested at all. During this time, the Duranies splintered up into side projects, Power Station and Arcadia (see sidebar). Meanwhile, "A View to a Kill," the title theme

to the James Bond movie, took the #1 spot in the United States. And in the summer of 1985, Duran Duran reconvened to play the instantly historic Live Aid benefit concert in Philadelphia.

Live Aid would be the last time the original fivesome played together, "which, I suppose, is a way to go out," Nick says. A year later, Roger left the group, and Andy soon followed suit, as did the group's long-standing managers, the Berrow brothers.

It would have been unrealistic to expect that the dizzying heights of fame, success, and carnal revelry generated by the teen-idol phenomenon could have been sustained past the mid-'80s.

Duran mania, as it was, lasted pretty long. But teens grow up, music skids in a different direction, and suddenly, without warning, girls prefer Bono and his mates as their poster boys du jour. It happens. But that doesn't negate the magic of the experience or erase the music. Because even now, there's still the music.

"You put 'Save a Prayer' on some beautiful music station," says Blade, "and it takes you back to that moment in time when these five guys walked on stage, the audience just exploded and you said, 'Wow, I wasn't there for the Beatles, but I was there for Duran Duran.'" ❀

> "Duran Duran is always **complete chaos.** *I don't know how it actually comes together. It's just like one of those molecules that you can never quite tie down.*"
> —NICK RHODES

CHAPTER 9

Menudo

Little Latin Lovers

> *"It was always run, run, run, run, hide, hide, run."*
> —ROBI ROSA

In the mid '80s, while teen sensations Tiffany and Debbie Gibson were getting their acts together in America's suburbs and New Kids on the Block were plotting out their dance moves in Beantown, there was another group of kids becoming legends south of the border. Menudo—a group of five boys from Puerto Rico—were stealing the hearts of girls all over Central and South America, long before they made their presence known Stateside. Menudo was the perfect construct for a pop phenomenon, the gimmick being that members were ousted when they reached the age of sixteen. Once a boy was beyond that age of innocence, he was replaced by a sweet-faced youngster, ready to please. So not only did band members rotate in and out but new fans jumped in as the years went on. All told, Menudo had thirty-three members in its twenty-year run and sold over twenty-five million albums.

"I was the biggest fan of Menudo. Menudo was a legend. Menudo united generations." —RICKY MARTIN

The original group—brothers Nefty and Fernando Sallaberry, and Carlos, Oscar, and Ricky Melendez—was created by Edgardo Diaz in 1977. "The concept of Menudo," Diaz says, "was that every time a kid reached a certain age, he had to leave the group. Once he looked too old, he had to leave." They became a pop sensation in Puerto Rico and released their first album, *Los Fantasmas.* By the end of the '70s, the founding lineup was already replaced by fresher-faced boys who kept the girls screaming.

KIKO AND THE MAN

Meanwhile, elsewhere in Puerto Rico, a nine-year-old who went by the nickname Kiko was getting his start in show business with TV commercials. "I was the biggest fan of Menudo. Menudo was a legend. Menudo united generations," says Kiko—today known to audiences near and far as Ricky Martin. By the time he was twelve, he was looking for a way to get his foot in the revolving Menudo door.

"I knew that there was a member that was leaving soon so I went to the office for an application," he says. "I filled it out and they called me a week later and gave me the audition." His credentials? "Good dancing, not too bad of a singer, and a little kid that really wanted it. I only had one problem—I was five feet tall."

A determined Ricky tried again six months later, but he hadn't grown enough. It was on his third audition that they finally gave him a shot. Manager and former Menudo choreographer Jose Luis Vega recalls, "We saw that he was all right—his charisma, his presence—that's what made us decide to put him in Menudo."

Ricky made his debut in the group in San Juan on July 10, 1984, just ten days after becoming a card-carrying member. Menudo at that time was Charlie Rivera, Ray Reyes, Roy Rosello, and Robi Rosa. Soon enough, the group took their act to the United States to test the waters there. They made their American debut with *Reaching Out,* which featured English versions of some of their most successful pop hits. Though they were never as big in the United States as they were in Latin American countries, their squeaky-clean image and boyish charm translated well, and they became international stars.

Menudo mania was at its peak. Robi Rosa recalls, "We'd be in some country where the Pope was going and then Menudo would show up, and it was more intense than when the Pope was around."

Ricky Martin agrees. "Sometimes it would get out of hand—and scary at times. But we loved it." And Johnny Lozada (1980–84, replaced by Robi) remembers the girls getting a little too close for comfort at concerts. "They got so excited. When I was little I used to have scratches all over my body." Miguel Cancel (1981–83), who went by the nickname Migue, confirms the insanity. "People running after you, cars following you, it felt like a dream world," he says.

But the bigger Menudo—the band, not the boys—got, the more they felt the pressures of success. It was a tightly run ship, where perfection and image were stressed. "I was trained to be a machine," Ricky says. "I was trained not to say, 'I cannot.' They tell you what to wear, what to sing, what kind of haircut—you completely lose perspective of what personality can be."

Says Robi, "People would get upset if you weren't smiling enough or if you didn't have the right getup, the right gear, didn't say the right things or you offended somebody's dog along the way. It was intense in that way." So intense that Robi became the first Menudo member to resign before his biological clock was up. Ricky, on the other hand, stayed for five years, retiring from the group in 1989 at the ripe old age of seventeen.

Menudo, however, continued recruiting new members until 1997.

A SONG CALLED "MARIA"

The biggest success story to come out of the Menudo experience was Ricky Martin.

After five years of shaking his underage bon-bon onstage, Ricky traveled to New York, and then to Mexico City, where he starred in a soap opera and acted in local theater. In 1991, Sony Music Mexico signed him to a record deal; he collaborated on his first two albums, *Ricky Martin* and *Me Amaras,* with Menudo alum Robi Rosa. The albums sold more than 1.5 million copies combined. Over the next couple of years, Ricky would add a stint on TV's *General Hospital* and Broadway's *Les Misérables* to his growing resume.

A song from Ricky's third album, *A Medio Vivir,* was just what he needed to push his solo stardom over the edge. "(Un Dos Tres) Maria," created with Robi Rosa, became a worldwide sensation in 1997, as much as Ricky's subsequent high-powered anthems, "The Cup of Life" and "Living La Vida Loca." In addition to his co-writing and producing duties on Ricky's projects, Robi also pursued a solo career. Both Ricky and Robi are proof that you can take the boy out of a band, but you can't take the music out of the boy. ✿

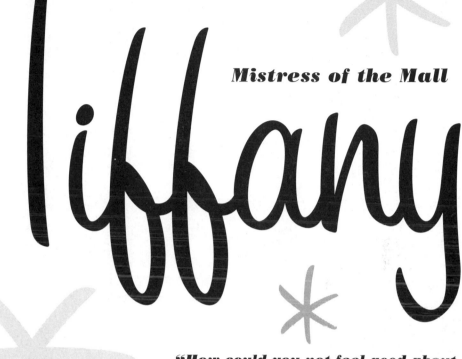

CHAPTER 10

Tiffany

Mistress of the Mall

*"How could you not feel good about
yourself or your music when you have
all these people screaming your name?"*

—TIFFANY

This is the story of the girl who could. From the time she was two, all little Tiffany Renee Darwish wanted to do was sing. For anyone. "I started playing at barbecues and hoedowns and fairs—anywhere they would have me." You name it, she played it. And from there she took it to the big time: the malls of America. It was an unlikely scheme to break a female teenage artist in a pre-Britney era, but a necessary one, and Tiffany was willing to do whatever it took to get her voice heard. In spite of a rocky childhood, a domineering manager, a tenuous relationship with her parents, and all the trials and tribulations of being a teen, Tiffany became a star.

So how exactly does a small-town girl from Southern California realize her dream of becoming a pop princess? Here's a tried and true plan, tested by '80s sensation Tiffany.

ONE: START YOUNG

"My mom and I were incredibly close when I was a little girl. In fact, she entered me into beauty contests, and I was a dancer from the time I was two years old. I did Tahitian dancing and tap and ballet. My mom really supported me and made all my costumes," says Tiffany. By the time she was ten, stepfather Dan Williams, with whom she had a shaky relationship (to put it mildly), started booking her locally in barbecues, picnics, and country-music festivals. Tiffany had a voice that could woo just about anyone away from their potato-sack races and apple pie. Folks started remembering her name.

But at home, the situation wasn't going quite as well. Money was an issue, and as it was, a lot was being poured into Tiffany's fledgling career. Tiffany's mom, Janie Williams, was drinking a lot, which led to fighting, chaos, and calls to the police. In 1983, when Tiffany was eleven, her stepfather took her two younger sisters to Oregon and filed for divorce. Janie checked herself into rehab, and would remain there until the following summer.

None of this put a halt to Tiffany's career. By this time, she already had a manager, Ron Surrett, and was dividing her time between him and the relatives who were looking after her. In the fall of 1983, Surrett bankrolled a recording session for Tiffany in the studio owned by producer George Tobin and his partner Brad Schmidt. The two were impressed by Tiffany's lungs. Unlike other teen performers who may have needed a little help when it came to laying down vocals, Tiffany was the real deal.

When Tiffany's mom returned home in the summer of 1984, they signed a contract with George Tobin, allowing him to take control of Tiffany's career. "I was signed directly to George," Tiffany says. "I was basically signed to him as his artist. So he had the right to go and sign to a label." He became her producer/manager, and Schmidt was co-manager. In no time, Tobin essentially took control of her life.

Says mom Janie, "I had no doubt in my mind that George could get her career going."

TWO: BE PERSISTENT

Now a bona fide recording artist, Tiffany put her nose to the grindstone, and Tobin held it firmly there. He searched out songs for her to cover, one of them being "I Think We're Alone Now," a Top Ten hit from 1967. According to Tiffany, Tobin kept her in the studio till all hours of the night—which led to many missed school days—to get the job done right. By the spring of 1986, Tobin and Schmidt had enough songs to hawk to record labels around Los Angeles, but they had no buyers. "No one wanted her," Tobin says. "And I'm talking about every record company you could possibly name at that time."

Then they turned the tables and had the labels come to them. Tiffany recalls, "Actually, we got our first record contract by having people come down to the studio and see me sing live to the tape. It was like a mini show-case. We'd have snacks in the studio and each label would come in and meet me a little bit and hear me sing live to four or five songs."

Executives from MCA Records loved what they heard. Larry Solters, a former vice president at the label, says, "Tiffany was well ahead of her years. It was hard to believe she was a fifteen-year-old with such poise, such presentation and such ability. She knocked us all out." Tiffany was signed right then and there.

Despite MCA's enthusiasm for the red-haired chanteuse, her songs collected dust on their shelves for months. Not quite sure how to market a teen artist in a time when the airwaves belonged to the likes of Lionel Richie and Huey Lewis and the News, MCA was in a lurch. Until Solters came up with the idea that would send her career through the roof: let Tiffany loose in the malls. Who shops at malls? Teens! Who's Tiffany's target audience? Teens! It made perfect sense. In the summer of 1986, fifteen-year-old Tiffany headlined a mall tour promoting a cosmetics company.

THREE: BUILD A FAN BASE (AND GET THEM TO ADORE YOU)

"I remember there were times that I was like, 'this is **really funky.** I feel really stupid.' But I love to sing, so it really didn't matter. I'd just go out there and I'd try it."

Tiffany's mall outings took a while to catch on, but as soon as people took a second to put down their Orange Julius and listen, an audience was born. "I started recognizing that something was happening when more and more people started coming," Tiffany says. "I'd get up onstage and there were hundreds of people. We always did the show and then went right to the record store to sign autographs—you know, buy an album and I'll sign it."

Soon enough, she'd built a following. Malls weren't just for shopping anymore; people were purposefully coming out to see Tiffany put on a show. Then, Tiffany says, "Radio changed everything. As they started playing 'I Think We're Alone Now,' people started to get familiar with the song. They would also sometimes announce the mall I was going to be at. And I would go and work radio and do the morning show, or any shows that I could do for them. It really started to build, people started to come out. That's when it became more fun for me, obviously, because I would meet people. There were a lot of times in between shows where I'd just go and have pizza."

After only weeks into the mall tour, Tiffany was drawing the fans in by the thousands. Teenage girls were eager to express their admiration. Tiffany recalls: "When we were doing Salt Lake City—and all the big malls, any double-decker mall—people were hanging banners over the side, and kind of hanging over the side to see me, and I'd wave up and talk a little bit more. It was really exciting. I mean, how could you not feel good about yourself or your music when you have all these people just screaming your name? And girls coming up to me going, 'I love your hair,' and I love this about you. I felt connected to my fans. I could completely relate to them because I wasn't raised with a silver spoon."

She says, "I always wanted to sign everything, meet everyone, and it was a really neat time, because I got to hear everybody go, 'I like your song.' 'You know, my sister and I dance in our room to it.'"

When the mall tour wound down in September 1987, Tiffany returned home, now a high school junior. While she cracked open her textbooks, her self-titled debut album was unleashed on the charts. She became close once again with her mother, and she even had a boyfriend. Two months after her record came out, though, it was anything but the status quo for this teenager. She was washing dishes one night when Tobin called her with phenomenal news: not only had "I Think We're Alone Now" hit #1 on the charts but it knocked Michael Jackson's "Bad" out of the slot to get there.

Tiffany traded in her knapsack for a suitcase and went on tour to support the album. By Christmas, she had a platinum hit on her hands.

FOUR: KEEP THE HITS COMING

Tiffany's second single, the sentimental ballad "Could've Been," climbed to #1 on the charts in February 1988. A gender-altered remake of a 1964 Beatles tune, "I Saw Him Standing There," earned a spot in the Top Ten. Yet, despite the fact that Tiffany's star was on the rise, things at home were becoming more and more complicated. For starters, Tiffany's mother began taking issue with the way Tobin was running her daughter's life. She was concerned that Tiffany was overworked for a teenager. Around the same time, Dan, Tiffany's stepfather, came back into the picture, which upset the pop star to no end.

In retrospect, Tiffany says, "All I wanted to do was get closer to my mom and have that same bonding and be able to talk to her. Then you add alcohol to that, and then you'd add statements from Dan's mouth,

like 'Well, if you ever get famous, [I'm] going to buy me a nice Cadillac.' I was just like, *oh no*. And that wasn't like, not with my money. That was like, I don't really like you—I'm not buying you anything."

Since she felt Dan's reappearance would only result in more of the chaos that was there the first time around, Tiffany gave her mother an ultimatum: him or me. Janie remarried Dan, and Tiffany fled.

Soon after, Tiffany took her mother to court in hopes of winning emancipation. Though she lost the case and had to pay her mother an allowance, she was permitted to move out of her parents' home. In the end, the case not only hurt her relationship with her mother but it also took its toll on her career. Fans saw her in a new, slightly unfavorable light: a teen idol *doesn't* take her parents to court, after all.

"I knew that it wasn't a good move on my part," Tiffany says. "I mean, here I am, the girl next door, and all of a sudden I'm suing my mother and having problems with my manager. He's being labeled as brainwashing this artist, and I'm looking like an idiot. That I'm being told to do everything, and I have no brain at all. That I'm a horrible person. That I'm a spoiled brat who basically thinks that she knows everything and is now depriving her parents of any kind of income."

Journalist Susan Orlean proposes that, "When you have a very public moment where you have a child star chafing at the authority of an adult, I think the innocence is gone."

Need proof? *Hold an Old Friend's Hand,* Tiffany's sophomore album, was released at the end of 1988. It sold only a third of what her first album did and spawned just one Top Ten hit for the songstress, "All This Time." Music fans were losing interest. "I could definitely tell that by the end of the first tour people were changing," Tiffany says. "The music was changing. On the radio I heard a lot of different styles of music. It was definitely way more dance. I had two dance songs—the rest were pretty mid-tempo adult songs, a lot of love songs actually. And the second album was really bubble-gum pop."

Tiffany was just not digging a lot of the music Tobin chose for her. "I remember being really upset about recording a lot of those songs. I came back to George and said 'Look, I'm out with the New Kids [on the Block], they're doing this great production, this great show, they've got these up-tempo songs and people are rocking out, and I'm coming out and bringing it down.' Because I was coming out and people were leaving. That was really crushing for me."

FIVE: BE TRUE TO YOURSELF

Okay, so there's a slight problem with "Four: Keep the Hits Coming." Teens are fickle, and when their tastes change, if you want more hits, you've got to grow with them. What's more is that teen idols of yore had very little control over their careers and what they sang. So when all else fails, you need a backup plan: Be true to yourself. Tiffany knew that music was "my gift and my calling. I felt so comfortable. When I was on that stage, that was the hour and a half that no one could touch me." But by 1989, it was getting harder and harder for her to settle for a paltry ninety minutes of peace.

So, says Tiffany, "I decided to sue George when I just wasn't able to get across to him anymore about my thoughts about the music. I was just miserable. And had compromised enough. I wasn't happy with the songs and he wasn't going to change.

"There was always a big compromise with my personality. And no amount of money meant anything to me for that." For the second time in her young life, eighteen-year-old Tiffany headed back to court to free herself of Tobin. When all was said and done, the girl who had earned herself a cool

"We weren't partners. Basically I was signed to him. I was basically his artist and there was nothing contractual that made me have any power to say, 'I don't want to do this.'"

few million bucks was no longer a millionaire. Freedom came with a high price tag.

In December 1990, under a new producer and new manager, Tiffany sent her third record out into the world, *A New Inside*. The fans who'd hung on her every note just three years earlier were no longer listening, and Tiffany was shattered. When her record went nowhere, she hid out for a while and developed a taste for pot. In the aftermath of her rise and fall from fame, she says, "For so many years I think I tried to run away from being young and being Tiffany, and being the mall girl, because I was a little embarrassed by it."

It didn't take long for her to get her life back on track. She married in 1992 and had a baby boy that same year. She's also repaired her relationship with her mother, and left the teen queen persona behind. The year 2000 saw the release of a new Tiffany album, *The Color of Silence*—done her way this time. When she talks about her pop-star stint in the '80s, she says, "It was like, 'be on top of the world'—kind of walking out and feeling everybody accepts this, everybody loves this music that I'm doing. You feel very special." With the stellar reviews her new album's gotten, chances are she feels the same way today.

❖

CHAPTER 11

"A guy jumped over the gate of our house and knocked on the door. Buck naked. I wasn't home—my grandmother opened the door." —DEBBIE

Out of the Electric Blue

Looking back, pop music in the late '80s was a murky thing. Madonna, U2, Michael Jackson, Whitney Houston, Guns N' Roses, and George Michael were among the heavy hitters on the charts, while acts as varied as Club Nouveau, the Escape Club, Rick Astley, Poison, Billy Ocean, and Atlantic Starr were able to carve their way into the #1 spot at least once. There wasn't exactly a movement in music to identify with—just pure pop power—which might explain how teen acts were able to step in and steal the spotlight for at least a little while. In 1987, out of this musical free-for-all came a girl from Long Island who was determined to shake our love and set new records in the music industry. That girl was Debbie Gibson.

Debbie was musically inclined from the get-go. As a child growing up in Merrick, New York, she got her start in community theatre at the tender age of five. She took piano lessons from Morton Estrin, who had also taught fellow Long Islander Billy Joel his way around the ivory. By six, Debbie was composing her own songs ("Make Sure You Know Your Classroom") and by eight, she'd made it to the famed Metropolitan Opera's Children's Chorus in New York City. When Debbie won a thousand dollars in a local songwriting contest with the tune "I Come from America" at age twelve, her parents decided it was time to find their pop prodigy a manager.

work or tuning into TV's *The Cosby Show,* Debbie was building a cottage industry of one in her garage.

Debbie's hard work paid off. At only sixteen, she was signed to Atlantic Records based on the strength of her demos. Still in school, Debbie recorded her first album, 1987's *Out of the Blue.* It was a collection of catchy, upbeat, optimistic tunes, and its first single, "Only in My Dreams," not only reached #4 on the pop chart but it made a splash on the dance chart as well. "Shake Your Love" also hit #4, just a month before so-called rival Tiffany's "I Think We're Alone Now" captured the #1 spot.

At the time, it was natural to draw comparisons between the two girls: only a year apart in age, they were both creating

Romance was the thing, not sex. And perhaps the better part of Debbie's appeal was the fact that she never stopped being a normal girl. She was the girl next door.

Under the wings of her manager, Doug Breithart, a thirteen-year-old Debbie honed her musical chops. She learned to write, arrange, and produce her own songs, and over the next three years she recorded more than a hundred demos at her home studio. While other kids at the time were doing home-

bubblegum music marketed expressly for teens. But like Christina Aguilera and Britney Spears today, they were cast into good-girl/bad-girl roles, with the floppy-hat-wearing Debbie playing the goody-goody to a brooding, dramatic Tiffany. Though they shared a similar sound—and both attracted a tremendous teen following—there was one thing they didn't share: the ability to take credit for their work. While Tiffany recorded tunes cherry-picked for success, Debbie wrote her own material.

"Beat" It

With the help of playful, teen-themed videos, Debbie's popularity continued to grow, and by May 1988, there was one more thing she could add to her successes. Her song "Foolish Beat" proved to be anything but that. When it went to #1, it made Debbie the youngest person ever to write, produce, and perform a single that made it all the way to #1 in the United States. Within a month, the wunderkind graduated from high school with honors and embarked on a U.S. tour. By the time her sophomore album, *Electric Youth*, came out in 1989, she was a full-fledged teen sensation.

She scored big with the syrupy ballad "Lost in Your Eyes" and the album's eponymous single. "Electric Youth" was a perky yet earnest appeal to take notice of a so-called teenage movement: *Electric youth / It's true you can't fight it / Live by it / The next generation...it's electric.* You could even smell the teen spirit— "Electric Youth" had its own fragrance. There was a certain innocence to Debbie's music that doesn't factor into the bubblegum

> ## "I would never disown what I've done. I'm not embarrassed by it. I'm exactly who I was, but older. There's no mystery."
>
> —DEBBIE

THE DAWN OF A NEW DEBORAH

Though *Anything Is Possible* spawned a couple of hits in 1990, it didn't reach the heights that Debbie's previous efforts had. She'd held onto her popularity for three years, and then it became time to move on—both for herself and her fans. Over the next eleven years, a more mature Deborah released six more albums—but her real achievement during that time was earned in the theater. She brought the house down on Broadway in *Les Misérables* and *Beauty and the Beast,* and in London's West End production of *Grease,* among other shows.

Like her 1980s teen-idol cohort Tiffany, Deborah released an album in the new millennium called *M.Y.O.B.,* or "Mind Your Own Business." Though she goes by the name Deborah now, she doesn't divorce herself of Debbie's past. "I would never disown what I've done," she once said. "I'm not embarrassed by it. I'm exactly who I was, but older. There's no mystery." She even admits to keeping some of her trademark hats on display, while the rest of the collection remain like innocent skeletons in her closet. This is not to say she's overly nostalgic about her teen years on top. "I [recently] met a casting director who said, 'You don't understand, I *am* an electric youth. And I was like, 'Get over it. You're in your thirties.'" Of all people, Deborah should know, you can't fight electric youth. ✿

of today. Romance was the thing, not sex. And perhaps the better part of Debbie's appeal was the fact that she never stopped being a normal girl. She *was* the girl next door. Hers was a homespun kind of success and didn't have the inaccessible quality that some of today's teen idols do. Whereas Christina, Britney, and Mandy Moore (though she has retained her adolescent sweetness) are superstars, Debbie was *just like you.*

THE NEW KIDS ARE ALRIGHT

What happens when boy bands break up? Or when one of the boys has a brother who wants to follow in his superstar steps? Simple: They get entered into the master list of Six Degrees of Boy Band Separation. Here are some of the more notable players.

New Kids on the Block (1984–94)

STARRING:
Donnie Wahlberg, Daniel Wood, Jordan Knight, Jonathan Knight, Joseph McIntyre

SOLO SPIN-OFFS:
Joey McIntyre, *Stay the Same* (1999); Jordan Knight, *Give It to You* (1999)

FAMILY TIES: Donnie's little brother, Mark Wahlberg (yes, the actor), hit it big with Marky Mark and the Funky Bunch's "Good Vibrations" (1991).

New Edition (1981–89)

STARRING: Bobby Brown, Ricky Bell, Ralph Tresvant, Michael Bivins, Ronald DeVoe

SOLO SPIN-OFFS: Bobby Brown, *King of the Stage* (1987) kicked off his prolific solo career; Ralph Tresvant, *Ralph Tresvant* (1990), *It's Goin' Down* (1994)

NEW ADDITION: *Provocative* solo artist Johnny Gill was brought in to replace Bobby Brown.

TRIPLE WHAMMY: Bell Biv DeVoe, *Poison* (1990), *Hootie Mack* (1993)

Take That (1990–96)

STARRING: Mark Owen, Robbie Williams, Gary Barlow, Howard Donald, Jason Orange

SOLO SPIN-OFFS: Gary Barlow, *Open Road* (1997), *Twelve Months Eleven Days* (2001); Robbie Williams, *Life Thru a Lens* (1997), *I've Been Expecting You* (1998), *The Ego Has Landed* (1999), *Sing When You're Winning* (2000)

Backstreet Boys (1993–present)

STARRING: Nick Carter, Howard Dorough, Kevin Richardson, AJ McLean, Brian Littrell

FAMILY TIES: Nick's little bro, Aaron Carter, stole the hearts of "tweens" with a remake of Bow Wow Wow's "I Want Candy."

CHAPTER 12

THE NEW KIDS, THE MONKEES, AND MORE

VITAL STATS: *New Kids on the Block*

NAMES:
Donnie Wahlberg, Daniel Wood, Jordan Knight, Jonathan Knight, Joseph McIntyre

GROUP BORN:
1984 in Boston

DISBANDED:
June 1994

STARR SEARCH:
Music mastermind Maurice Starr put the group of white boys together in an effort to duplicate the success of his all-black creation, New Edition.

FIRST SINGLE:
"Be My Girl"

DISCOGRAPHY:
New Kids on the Block (1986)
Hangin' Tough (1988)
Step by Step (1990)
Face the Music (1994)

FIRST TOUR:
Opening act for Tiffany during her 1988 tour. Halfway through, Tiffany was demoted to second billing and the New Kids headlined.

NEW KIDS IN THE BUCKS:
The kids topped the *Forbes* list of highest-paid entertainers when their earnings for 1990–91 rang in at $115 million. Lesser paid celebs included Bill Cosby, Oprah Winfrey, Michael Jackson, and Madonna.

IS DONNIE THERE?
In a pre-Internet era, the fans could dial up the Kids to hear a recorded message. At one point, 1-900-909-5 KIDS reportedly received upward of 125,000 calls a day.

NAME CHANGE:
The kids, not so new anymore, officially became NKTOB in 1992.

ONCE MORE AROUND THE BLOCK:
Joey McIntyre—now Joey Mac—plays the sleazy Vegas host of MTV's *Say What? Karaoke*. His solo album *Stay the Same* was released in 1999. Jordan Knight returned in 1999 with *Give It to You*, written and produced by Jimmy Jam and Terry Lewis.

VITAL STATS: *Shaun Cassidy*

BIRTHDAY:
September 27, 1958

HOMETOWN:
Los Angeles

FAMOUS PARENTS:
Jack Cassidy (actor) and Shirley Jones
(actress/singer)

FAMOUS SIBLING:
Half brother David Cassidy

FIRST TASTE OF SUCCESS:
Shaun was initiated to the ranks of
idoldom in Europe and Australia before
hitting it big in the United States, thanks
to his hits "Morning Girl" and "That's Rock
'n' Roll," an Eric Carmen cover.

NONSENSICAL #1 TITLE:
The wholesome-looking heartthrob
became a household name with a cover
of the Crystals' "Da Do Ron Ron," which
went to #1 in 1977.

DISCOGRAPHY:
Shaun Cassidy (1977);
Born Late (1977); *Under Wraps* (1978);
Room Service (1979); *That's Rock 'n' Roll:
Shaun Cassidy Live* (1979);
Wasp (1980)

ALSO SEEN IN:
Though he had several albums attached
to his name, Shaun remained a one-hit
wonder. It was his role as Joe Hardy in
TV's *The Hardy Boys Mysteries* (1977–79)
that kept Shaun a fixture on bedroom
walls and pillowcases. He also appeared
on *General Hospital* (see "The Men of
Daytime TV," page 45).

SIBLING REVELRY:
In 1993, Shaun and David appeared
on the Broadway stage together in
Blood Brothers.

VITAL STATS: *The Bay City Rollers*

ORIGINAL LINEUP:
Derek Longmuir, Alan Longmuir, Les McKeown, Stuart "Woody" Wood, Eric Faulkner

BAND BORN:
1967 in Edinburgh, Scotland

R.I.P.:
They parted ways in 1978.

WHAT'S IN A NAME:
Originally dubbed the Saxons, the Rollers chose their name by choosing a locale at random from the United States map.

TRADEMARK OUTFIT:
Tartan plaid. It drove the girls wild. Says Les McKeown, "For a couple of years all the teenagers in this country wore a tartan outfit, and if you didn't have one, you were nobody."

FIRST SINGLE:
"Keep On Dancing"

FIRST #1:
"Saturday Night"

NONSENSICAL HIT TITLE:
"Shang-a-Lang" was not only a song but a weekly TV variety show that debuted in April 1975. By that time, they were a fully blown marketing success story. Their faces were plastered on merchandise around the world.

THE CURSE OF THE IDOLS:
The Rollers maintain that their every move was controlled by manager Tam Paton. By spring 1975, at the peak of their career, they were also feeling the burn of the teen idol spotlight. Drummer Derek Longmuir says, "It was very difficult just to get away from it all and get some peace. Everywhere we went, we were recognized."

UNRESOLVED SCANDAL:
When the mania subsided, the Scottish lads found out that their fortunes had been tied up in several untraceable accounts. To this day, the former Bay City Rollers are unable to get their hands on their money.

VITAL STATS:
The Monkees

NAMES:
Michael Nesmith, Peter Tork,
Davy Jones, Micky Dolenz

GROUP ASSEMBLED:
1965 in Los Angeles

LAST TRAIN TO SPLITSVILLE:
1969

PREFAB FOUR:
The group was made for TV in an effort to
capitalize on the Beatles' success with
preteen girls (think: *A Hard Day's Night*).
Like the Partridge Family after them, they
were a group solely assembled for TV
ratings, not record sales. Session musicians
were called in to perform on their first two
records, much to the Monkees' dismay.
The bulk of the material came from
Tommy Boyce, Bobby Hart, Carole King,
Gerry Goffin, and Neil Diamond.

SERIES RUN:
September 1966 to March 1968

FIRST SINGLE:
"Last Train to Clarksville" snagged the #1 spot on the charts in September 1966.

CHART TOPPERS:
"I'm a Believer" and "Daydream Believer" both went to #1, while "A Little Bit Me, A Little Bit You," "Pleasant Valley Sunday," and "Valleri" all made it to the Top Ten.

BRUSH WITH CREDIBILITY:
Starred with Frank Zappa in the pop-culture flick *Head* (1968), which was co-written and co-produced by Jack Nicholson. If that's not mind-blowing enough, a virtually unknown Jimi Hendrix opened up for the Monkees on their 1967 U.S. tour. Thankfully, for everyone involved, that arrangement was remedied after a few shows.

THE OL' TEEN IDOL CATCH-22:
Though their reason for being was the television show, the Monkees were frustrated that they weren't allowed to play their own instruments or write the music themselves. With 1967's *Headquarters,* they were finally able to get their hands dirty and record their own work. ✿

CHAPTER 13

BOYS VS. GIRLS
BATTLE
OF THE BANDS

Every generation has its own Donny, its own David, its own Duran Duran.

With the teen-idol floodgates propped open by the late '80s, a new crop of pubescent pop stars poured in and took control over new sets of hearts, new bedroom walls, and new plastic wallets. Tiffany, Debbie Gibson, and the New Kids on the Block were proof not only that kids needed their idols but that they'd put their money where their fan-club cards were. But pop music tends to go in cycles, and by the early '90s it had fallen out of favor when modern rock made its presence known.

Then in 1996, while post-grunge alternative music was burying its head in the sand, pop music sauntered back in to steal the show. The Hanson boys and the Spice Girls got our attention, and while we were trying to figure out what it was they were saying, the Britneys, the Christinas, and the Backstreets snuck in and took the stage. If grunge music was a plaintive cry from the depths of an economic recession, this new era of bubblegum was egged on by a sweet outlook and big bucks. The kids had arrived.

And they're still here. Just when you think it's over, the pop-star cookie-cutter offers up another girl singer whose name ends in *y* to expose her midriff and take things to the next level. Or a group of boys who only *look* like they're under twenty-one materialize as if from an assembly line to perform great dance moves and harmonize on songs about angels, first loves, and broken hearts. As long as teenage consumers have the money to spend, the carbon keeps making copies.

Let's face it: pop is in high demand. This time around, the teen idols are savvier, sexier, and more sugary than ever before. Thanks to music video, and shows such as MTV's *Total Request Live,* where the countdown is in the hands of the viewers, the teen dream is burning bright. So here's a look at some of its more influential headliners.

FIRST SINGLE:
"...Baby One More Time"

DISCOGRAPHY:
...*Baby One More Time* (1999; debuted at #1); *Oops!...I Did It Again* (2000); sold over one million albums the first week—this is where she takes "it" to the next level); *Britney* (2001).

BIBLIOGRAPHY:
Britney Spears's Heart to Heart, a memoir cowritten with her mom

PETS:
Baby, a Yorkshire terrier

RUMOR THAT WON'T DIE:
That her breasts are surgically enhanced.

PROOF IT'S NOT TRUE:
Did you see her stage show at the 2000 *MTV Video Music Awards?* It left little doubt that she's all real.

PERFECT BOYFRIEND:
"Someone who has a wonderful personality, who can make me laugh. That's a must. I love to laugh. And someone who loves me for me, and not just for what I do."

FIND HER ONLINE @:
www.britneyspears.com
The site even features "Lynne's Corner," an online journal penned by the starlet's mother that lets fans know what's going on with "Brit."

ENOUGH SAID:
"I was going through a stage about six months ago where...I was listening to my mind all the time and I forgot about my soul."

NAME:

Britney Jean Spears

BIRTHDAY:
December 2, 1981

HOMETOWN:
Kentwood, Louisiana

DEBUT:
TV's *Mickey Mouse Club* at age eleven, breeding ground for up-and-comers like Christina Aguilera, J.C. Chasez, and Justin Timberlake.

GOT OUR ATTENTION:
... by wearing pigtails and a strategically adjusted Catholic schoolgirl uniform in her first video.

NAME:

Christina Maria Aguilera

BIRTHDAY:
December 18, 1980

HOMETOWN:
Staten Island, New York

DEBUT:
Star Search, age eight (she lost)

STAR TURN:
Christina sang "Reflection" for
Disney's *Mulan*

TEEN-IDOL ARCHETYPE:
She's a feisty Tiffany to Britney's
Debbie Gibson.

FIRST SINGLE:
"Genie in a Bottle"

DISCOGRAPHY:
Christina Aguilera (1999); *Mi
Reflejo* (2000); *My Kind of
Christmas* (2000)

**SONG YOU
CAN'T GET OUT
OF YOUR HEAD:**
"What a Girl Wants" (See?
Now you can't, can you?)

**WELCOME
TO THE CLUB:**
Christina won a Grammy for
Best New Artist in 2000.

CATFIGHT: With rapper
Eminem over a ribald comment he
made about her in one of
his songs.

FIND HER ONLINE @:
www.christina-a.com
Includes "Ask Shelly!," where fans can
e-mail the pop-star's mom questions about
her little girl. Also check out the "Rumor
Mill"—a section devoted to addressing,
debunking, and confirming such issues
as Christina's dress size (2), eye contact
(she makes it), and her height and weight
(5'2" and 102 lbs.), among juicier items.

ENOUGH SAID:
"Over the past year, I've really gotten to
know myself because in interviews I'm
constantly asked to look at myself, what
I'm about, what I want. It keeps me in
check with me...."

Backstreet Boys

NAMES:

Nickolas Gene Carter, Howard Dwaine Dorough (aka Howie D), Kevin Scott Richardson, Alexander James McLean (AJ), Brian Littrell

GROUP BORN:

1993 in Orlando, Florida

BOYS TO MEN:

The youngest member (Nick) was born in 1980; the oldest (Kevin) in 1971. Two (Brian and Kevin) are married.

FIRST SINGLE:

"Quit Playing Games (With My Heart)"

DISCOGRAPHY:

Backstreet Boys (1996); *Millennium* (1999, debuted at #1 and sold a then-record 1.13 million copies the first week alone); *Christmas Album* (1999); *Black & Blue* (2000)

BSB MANIA:

When the group debuted the video for "Shape of My Heart" on MTV's *TRL* in October 2000, more than six thousand fans came out to scream their lungs out in Times Square. NYC had to declare a state of emergency in the area.

AJ'S FAVORITE FOOD:

The fast kind.

HOWIE D'S DREAM DATE:

According to the Web site, this Romeo is partial to a candlelight dinner, followed by a movie or dancing, ending with a long walk on the beach.

NICK'S KIN:

Little brother is preteen idol Aaron Carter.

FIRST TASTE OF FAN WORSHIP:

Brian recalls his first show as a BSB— "We performed a fifteen-minute set at SeaWorld in Orlando for five thousand eighth graders and the crowd went crazy. I felt like a big shot with girls chanting my name and asking me for autographs."

FIND THEM ONLINE @:

www.backstreetboys.com

In addition to news and band information, the site features the boys' bios with their likes, dislikes, and ideal girls. Whose favorite actor is Jeff Goldblum? Who appeared in the movie *Cop and a Half*? Whose idea of a perfect date is "Whatever her heart desires"? Log on to find out. If you still have questions, send them an email at *backstreetboys@firmentertainment.net*.

*NSYNC

NAMES:

James Lance Bass, Joshua Scott Chasez, Joseph Anthony Fatone Jr., Christopher Alan Kirkpatrick, Justin Randall Timberlake

YOU CAN CALL THEM:

Lance, JC, Joey, Chris, and Justin

GROUP BORN:

1995 in Orlando, Florida

MANBAND?:

Justin, the youngest, was born in 1981; Chris, the elder tribesman, was born in 1971.

FIRST SINGLE:

"I Want You Back"

DISCOGRAPHY:

*NSYNC (1998); *Home for Christmas* (1998); *No Strings Attached* (2000); *Celebrity* (2001)

KICKED SOME BACKSTREET BUTT:

...when *No Strings Attached* sold 2.42 million copies in its first week out—breaking the BSB record of 1.thirteen million for *Millennium*'s first seven days.

BOY BAND POINT OF DIFFERENTIATION:

JC says, "What makes us special is that we sing love songs, but we throw people off guard because we're in your face. So many boy bands just sing about meeting the coolest girl, but to me, that's not the way to go, man. Don't just be a dude in a club picking up chicks."

...FOR EXAMPLE:

"God Must Have Spent a Little More Time on You" (How in-your-face sweet is that?)

BOY BAND POINT OF SIMILARITY:

Both the Backstreet Boys and *NSYNC got their feet off the ground with the help of teen idol-maker Louis Pearlman—someone who obviously knows what a girl wants. Since hitting it big, both supergroups have emancipated themselves from the impresario with out-of-court settlements, and both are currently on the Jive label.

FIND THEM ONLINE @:

www.nsync.com

While some fans are satisfied with buy, buy, buying basic memorabilia like posters, charm bracelets, board games, and lunch boxes, others can indulge their passions for all things *NSYNC with exclusive 20" marionettes. It's three hundred bucks a boy, strings attached.

NAMES:
Melanie Janine Brown (Mel B.), Melanie Jayne Chisholm (Mel C), Victoria Caroline Beckham, Geraldine Estelle Halliwell, Emma Lee Bunton

ALTER-EGOS:
Scary Spice, Sporty Spice, Posh Spice, Ginger Spice, Baby Spice

GROUP BORN:
1994 in London, England

FIRST SINGLE:
"Wannabe"

DISCOGRAPHY:
Spice (1996); *Spiceworld* (1997); *Forever* (2000)

BIBLIOGRAPHY:
Forever Spice, 2000; *Girl Power!*, 1997

FILM CREDITS:
Spiceworld: The Movie, 1997

FELL OFF THE SPICE RACK:
Ginger defected in May 1998

CATCHPHRASE THAT GAVE "MMMBOP" A RUN FOR ITS MONEY:
"Zigazig-ha"

BIGGER THAN JESUS, BEATLES:
The girls were the first act in U.K. chart history to have their first four singles hit #1 ("Wannabe," "Say You'll Be There," "2 Become 1," and "Who Do You Think You Are")

HIS ROYAL HEINIE:
During a meet-and-greet with Prince Charles, a naughty Spice Girl was said to have pinched His Highness's bum.

U.N.-SPICE:
Former member Geri Halliwell boasts the title of Goodwill Ambassador to the United Nations.

SOLO SPICE:
Critics did back flips for Mel C.'s 1999 effort, *Northern Star.* Unfortunately, listeners weren't hooked on *Schizophonic*, Geri's 1999 solo album.

FIND THEM ONLINE @:
www.spicegirlsforever.co.uk

Spice Girls

NAMES:
Clarke Isaac Hanson, Jordan Taylor Hanson, Zachary Walker Hanson

GROUP BORN:
1992 in Tulsa, Oklahoma

BROTHERS BORN:
Isaac, 1980; Taylor, 1983; Zac, 1985

DEBUT:
Tulsa's Mayfest Celebration

FIRST SINGLE:
"MMMBop"

ARRIVAL SIGNALED:
The end of grunge angst.

DISCOGRAPHY:
Middle of Nowhere (1997); *Snowed In* (1997); *Live from Albertane* (1998); *This Time Around* (2000)

CREDITED WITH:
Putting the "teen" back in teen pop—the boys nearly triple-handedly cleared the way for the teen-idol craze that began in the late '90s.

KIDSTUFF:
The video for "MMMBop" featured the threesome playing around on skateboards, scooters, and bikes, unabashedly celebrating their prepubescence.

SECOND TIME AROUND:
After a three-year hiatus between their first and second albums, the band not only acquired an extra foot or so in height but also the kind of critical acclaim and credibility that so many teen acts lack. Their sophomore outing had an evolved sound, separating them from the teeny-bopper pack.

TRADEMARK LOOK:
Long blond tresses.

BOY BAND POINT OF DIFFERENTIATION:
They play their own instruments.

FIND THEM ONLINE @:
www.hansonline.com

Hanson

DEAR DONNY...

Keeping up with those objects of obsession couldn't be easier these days, thanks to the Internet. If you want to find out what's going on with some of the artists in the book, check out these Web sites.

Christina Aguilera

christina-a.com

WRITE TO:
The Official Christina Aguilera Fan Club
P.O. Box 1396
Wexford, PA 15090-1396

Backstreet Boys

backstreetboys.com

The Beatles

thebeatles.com

David Cassidy

davidcassidy.com

Duran Duran

duranduran.com
johntayloronline.com

Deborah Gibson

deborah-gibson.com

Hanson

hansonline.com

Ricky Martin

rickymartin.com

*NSYNC

nsync.com

WRITE TO:
The *NSYNC Official
International Fan Club
P.O. Box 5248
Bellingham, WA 98227

Donny Osmond

donny.com

WRITE TO:
Donny Osmond
51 W Center St. #424
Orem, UT 84057

Elvis Presley

elvis.com

Britney Spears

britneyspears.com

WRITE TO:
Britney Beat
Dept. Fan Mail
P.O. Box 192730
San Francisco, CA 94119-2730

Spice Girls

spicegirlsforever.co.uk

Rick Springfield

rickspringfield.com

WRITE TO:
Rick Springfield
Box #106
30765 Pacific Coast Highway
Malibu, CA 90265

Tiffany

tiffanymusic.com

**Look for these
other titles
from VH-1 /
Pocket Books**

BEHIND THE MUSIC™

Behind the Music Willie Nelson

Behind the Music
The Day the Music Died

Available from VH-1
Pocket Books
Trade Paperbacks
www.SimonSays.com
www.vh1.com

Behind the Music
Casualties of Rock

Behind the Music 1968